The 12 Attributes
of Extraordinary
Media Professionals

Praise for *The 12 Attributes of Extraordinary Media Professionals*

"From the 'little things' to the big picture, Roger Cooper's *12 Attributes of Extraordinary Media Professionals* offers students and media professionals in any stage of their careers practical advice and tips for developing the soft skills so critical to success. I plan on adopting it for the leadership seminar I'm teaching."
—Marianne Barrett, Arizona State University

"The twelve attributes Cooper details in his book are applicable to career development stemming from organic human needs. Not only are they a great guide for attaining a career in the film industry, but they are also a great guide for creating a career you are happy to wake up to every day, surrounded by people with ethics similar to your own. As with all our choices along life's journey, we create more of what we pursue, and this perspective is invaluable for joy in the field, for the long haul."
—Reena Dutt, producer, actor, director

"Cooper has written an extremely valuable and timely book. His exploration of the attributes we continually work to develop in our students is done with illustrative stories, wisdom, and humor. This book should be required reading for every student who aspires to a career as a media professional."
—Robin Howard, director, Syracuse University LA Semester

"What are the characteristics that propel some to long-term success while other equally talented people fail? *The 12 Attributes of Extraordinary Media Professionals* is like a checklist for success. Since reading it, I see proof of these ideas repeatedly in the people I work with and in my own career. I can't recommend it enough."
—Dan O'Shannon, Emmy-winning writer/producer

"I've worked with hundreds of students from colleges and universities across the nation, encouraging them to dream big and pursue those dreams with confidence. Cooper's *12 Attributes of Extraordinary Media Professionals* is a stabilizing must-read for anyone starting a career in media."
—Nancy Robinson, director of education programs, Television Academy Foundation

"*The 12 Attributes of Extraordinary Media Professionals* is informative, inspiring, and much needed in our field. Cooper 'speaks' directly with readers, often with a great sense of humor. Readers will not feel like they're reading a book, but rather engaging with a caring mentor. This is a book written from the heart of a true educator and will capture the heart of its readers. As a media professor, I'm excited to adopt this book in my classes."
—Tang Tang, Kent State University

"Roger Cooper without a doubt knows the qualities one needs to succeed at their craft. I've experienced his gentle yet passionate way with students firsthand. Now everyone can experience the Roger Cooper way. I highly recommend it."
—Herb Trawick, creator and co-host, *Pensado's Place*

The 12 Attributes
of Extraordinary
Media Professionals

Roger Cooper

Ohio University

ROWMAN & LITTLEFIELD
Lanham • Boulder • New York • London

Credits and acknowledgments for material borrowed from other sources, and reproduced with permission, appear on the appropriate pages within the text.

Published by Rowman & Littlefield
An imprint of The Rowman & Littlefield Publishing Group, Inc.
4501 Forbes Boulevard, Suite 200, Lanham, Maryland 20706

www.rowman.com

86-90 Paul Street, London EC2A 4NE, United Kingdom

British Library Cataloguing in Publication Information Available

Library of Congress Cataloging-in-Publication Data
Names: Cooper, Roger, 1961– author.
Title: The 12 attributes of extraordinary media professionals / Roger Cooper.
Other titles: Twelve attributes of extraordinary media professionals
Description: Lanham : Rowman & Littlefield, [2022] | Includes bibliographical
    references and index. | Summary: "Few future media professionals understand
    that personal attributes like adaptability and integrity are just as important as
    industry knowledge. This book combines examples of successful professionals
    with activities to begin readers' development of attributes that will remain
    relevant despite career-stage or future technological development"—Provided by
    publisher.
Identifiers: LCCN 2021014403 (print) | LCCN 2021014404 (ebook) | ISBN
    9781538116265 (cloth) | ISBN 9781538116272 (paperback) | ISBN
    9781538116289 (epub)
Subjects: LCSH: Mass media—Vocational guidance—United States. | Mass media—
    Moral and ethical aspects—United States.
Classification: LCC P91.6 .C3767 2022 (print) | LCC P91.6 (ebook) |
    DDC 302.2302/3—dc23
LC record available at https://lccn.loc.gov/2021014403
LC ebook record available at https://lccn.loc.gov/2021014404

♾™ The paper used in this publication meets the minimum requirements of
American National Standard for Information Sciences—Permanence of Paper for
Printed Library Materials, ANSI/NISO Z39.48–1992.

Dedicated to
Patricia Cooper
My light from above

Brief Contents

Contents

The 13th Attribute Luck 147

Preface

A simple question changed my professional life.

In 2000, successful media professionals from around the United States came to my university for a day-long alumni conference. Some of these former students had graduated only a year or two earlier, while others had been media professionals for twenty years. I had taught some of these professionals in my classes, but others I met for the first time. The interests and professional positions covered a range of the media industries. Some worked in strictly "creative" positions, such as writers, directors, and performers, while others worked more on the business side, such as production managers or in sales, marketing, promotion, and finance at a major Hollywood studio.

During these seminar sessions, I listened to numerous stories (often painful, but never boring) about the struggles our graduates had undertaken to find work and to gain a foothold in the profession. For some, simply finding *any* job related to media took months of hard work, followed by months, even years, of low pay. Some had developed a specific technical skill while in school, such as operating a camera or editing, and continued to use that skill in the industry. Some others had displayed no direct interest in a specific skill while in college but had taken positions that were now highly technical in nature. Others had gravitated into areas unrelated to their interests while in college. Still others did not major in our media program, and they, too, were building successful careers. I also realized that a sizeable percentage of our graduates, excellent students and people, never found entry into any part of the business and moved into entirely different professions. I had lost track of many of them. I wondered if they were "happy" with what they are doing now.

As these individuals enthusiastically offered advice to our current students about how to navigate the media professions, I looked at our program's most successful professionals and played a kind of game ascribing "reasons" behind these individual successes. I soon determined, at least with my school's graduates, that effective navigation through a highly competitive, broad set of industries couldn't be pinpointed solely to grade point average (GPA), intelligence, our curriculum, innate artistic talent, or a specific technical skill. Although I couldn't yet put my finger on it, there seemed to be a link missing between what our graduates "knew," what marketable skills they might "have," and how they might traverse most effectively *long term* through these professions. But what was the missing link?

Near the end of the day's last session, composed of more experienced media professionals, I finally spoke up. "What would you tell our current students *are the most important qualities for success*?" I wrote the following responses on my gray notepad: "passion"; "ability to communicate"; "flexibility"; "persistence"; "problem-solver"; "good connections"; "thick skin"; "drive"; "well rounded"; and "willingness to learn."

These answers fascinated me. We rarely, if ever, teach these concepts in our classes, I thought, and yet *these* are the qualities most important for success?!?

We teach the hard skills, like editing software or physical production; we give our students specific experiences behind and in front of the camera or a microphone; and we mix in critical analysis and media management. But we almost never formally address what these successful working professionals said were most important for success.

I became captivated with this idea. At various national media industry conferences, or whenever film producers and directors, journalists, casting agents, music producers, and TV executives visited the school, I would eagerly speak up and ask professionals to describe "what is most important" to achieve success. The answers remained remarkably consistent. Rarely were specific technical or "hard" skills mentioned, even among those who depended heavily on hard skills to do their work. The broader "soft skills" were readily offered up as the more important reasons for success.

My emerging interest, sparked by my question at that alumni conference, drove me to find ways to help future professionals navigate their careers while continuing to learn and observe—and make distinctions—about what it takes to successfully navigate a career in media-related professions. Nearly 1,200 media professionals responded to a lengthy survey I developed to assess what professionals believe are important attributes for success. More than 300 of them requested a copy of the results, a good sign that I might be on to something.

I continued to seek more insights as I started a Los Angeles (LA) program that began as an intensive one-week excursion and then expanded into semester- and summer-long experiences that included internships that I directly oversaw. The LA programs were heavily populated with guest speakers from the industry who continued to lend insights, experiences, and new distinctions about the important qualities needed for success.

For two years, I led an institute at Ohio University sponsored by the National Association of Broadcasters. Recent college graduates from around the Midwest were trained in an intensive two-week workshop by professional leaders in marketing, human resources, persuasion, and station management. I continued to ask these successful leaders about the qualities needed for success.

I read books and articles about individuals who are widely considered successful and spoke with top leaders in media from around the United States. Each had a unique story of entry into television or music or film or digital or some related area of media. I explored research connected to the concepts that successful professionals identified as important to success. This engagement further illuminated why these qualities might foster success in media professions.

All of these various insights provided clues to help aspiring professionals make it into and "up" these various industries. Through this process, I came to the conclusion that media professionals need an inordinately large array of personal attributes that fall outside (or beyond) what we traditionally teach in the classroom. We (i.e., teachers and media professionals) *want* these "good" attributes for the people in our work lives, but few of us seem to teach them or to articulate their importance. We want a greater number of aspiring and young professionals to be passionate, to show an abundant curiosity, and to be "ready" to deal with the bumps on the road to success. We recognize that graduation from college might be the end of one's formal education but is near the beginning of one's education in the media business—and *life*. What if we are able to articulate a set of attributes that can significantly enhance success over the long term?

What has ensued for me since I first asked my simple question is hundreds of new relationships, deep learning, and important new insights about the media professions—and life itself.

I hope the distinctions you make will enhance your life, too.

Navigating the Challenges to Long-Term Success

In the documentary *Comedian*, Jerry Seinfeld stands offstage at a New York City comedy club with Orny Adams, a younger comic working his way up. Orny expresses concern about whether he has chosen the right profession.

"I get to the point where I wonder how much longer can I take it," Orny says.

Jerry clearly doesn't understand Orny's predicament. "What's wrong, time running out?" Jerry asks. "You out of time?"

"I'm getting older," Orny replies. "I'm 29. I feel like I've sacrificed so much of my life. The last three years have been like a blur."

"Is there something else you'd rather do? You got other appointments or places you've got to be?"

"I see my friends making a lot of money on Wall Street," Orny continues. "My friends are moving up."

Jerry is incredulous, completely perplexed by what he is hearing.

"Moving up? Are you outta your mind!?! This has nothing to do with your friends." Jerry then motions toward the stage. "This is such a special thing."

But Orny presses on. "Did you ever stop and compare your life. . . . My friends are all married, all have kids, they all have houses." Seinfeld's face contorts like he's eaten a bitter fruit that he's trying to spit out. "They have some sense of normality. What do you tell your parents?"

"Your *parents*!?!" Seinfeld then falls across a table, shakes his head while breaking out into laughter founded in disbelief.

Jerry rises up, pulls himself together, and proceeds to tell Orny a story:

"This is my favorite story about show business. Glenn Miller's orchestra is playing somewhere and they can't land where they're supposed to land because of a winter snowy night. So they land in a field and have to walk to the gig. They're dressed in their suits and they're ready to play, carrying their instruments, so they're walking through the snow and it's wet and it's slushy, and in the distance they see this little house. There's lights on inside, a billow of smoke coming out of the chimney. They go up to the house and they look in the window and they see this family. It's a guy, his wife—she's beautiful—two kids, they're all sitting around the table and they're smiling, they're laughing and they're eating. There's a fire in the fireplace. These guys are standing there in their suits, they're wet and shivering and holding their instruments and they're watching this incredible Norman Rockwell scene. And one guy turns to the other guy and says, 'How do people live like *that*?' That's what it's about."

Of course, Jerry Seinfeld's story about Glenn Miller's orchestra does not apply merely to stand-up comedy or big bands but to the entire range of media and creative industries, whether it is film, television, recording, journalism, publishing, and the vast array of creative and business positions within and across these industries. The pathways into and ascension up any and all of these industries are rarely easy, linear, or predictable. But if you're reading this book, I assume that you seek things other than a nine-to-five Norman Rockwell existence. The media and creative industries are not "built" for that, and the prospect of what might ensue excites you, even if the unknown feels a bit scary at times. You are guided by a value system different from what's found in most other professions, as others you know (including loved ones) may not understand "why" you strive toward the dreams you have. You may feel implicit or explicit pressure to assume a more "normal" existence as you look around and see others with more stable pathways.

Not that there's anything wrong with that, as Seinfeld might say.

But *you* seek something more. You are driven by the opportunity to be involved in some part of the storytelling process. You are attracted to the allure of creating *content* that will affect viewers, listeners, readers, or users in some way. You are drawn toward, even passionate about, devoting your time and energies toward a lifestyle instead of a punch clock. You want to get paid for doing something you love.

That's great, but there's a catch.

I've discovered during more than twenty-five years of observing young and aspiring professionals that few are prepared for the degree of challenges they will face. Part of the reason is that those who are successful in media make it look exciting and easy. But it takes a lot of hard work to make something *look* effortless, so it is easy to believe that "anyone" can do this. The reality is that not "anyone" can do this well and the level of competition is such that even some who may do it well will not receive opportunities to do this work. Jerry Seinfeld might make stand-up comedy, sitcom stardom, authorship, and digital content (*Comedians in Cars Getting Coffee*) look easy, but one viewing of *Comedian* will clearly drive home the intense effort it takes to gain and maintain a position of prominence in media-related professions.

Oprah Winfrey makes it look easy. If you know her story, you know she endured enormous challenges before creating her own extraordinary pathway. Raised poor, black, and female in rural Mississippi, Oprah could hardly have entered the world in more bleak circumstances. She spent her childhood being shuttled between families, suffered sexual abuse, and was constantly told that her dreams were stupid. But she discovered that she had a knack for public speaking and decided she wanted to be "paid to talk." With few women of color as role models in television, Oprah forged her own pathway, ignoring the whisperers, using naysayers to fuel her ambitions, self-belief, and resilience against high odds. Oprah is not *Oprah* because she had an easy pathway or didn't work to develop her talents, but rather because she accessed key qualities that connected to people in an extraordinary way.

Quentin Tarantino makes it look easy. If you were to judge him from the popular press, you might think Tarantino went from working at a video store to make *Reservoir Dogs* (only a minor exaggeration), which led to *Pulp Fiction* and an extraordinary career in filmmaking. This quick and clean path provides a nice "hook" and the industry's marketing machinery encourages this simplistic storytelling. The press can't convey the intense passion that Tarantino applied to put himself into position to influence a generation of aspiring filmmakers. The secret to Tarantino's success is not that he "fell" into filmmaking, but rather that he internalized a set of values to such a degree that his efforts were, in fact, effortless *to him*. This accelerated the pace of his progression, perhaps, but the process existed nonetheless.

Lady Gaga, however, does *not* make it look easy. She was told she was "too unconventional" and heard "no" enough to last a lifetime. A survivor of sexual assault who openly struggles with mental health issues, Gaga's grit and uncompromising honesty created a uniquely extraordinary path. She resourcefully owned who she is to become a music superstar, actress, and the first woman to win Academy, Grammy, BAFTA, and Golden Globe awards in the same year. Suffering chronic pain from fibromyalgia, Gaga nevertheless uses her platform to promote mental health, equality, and diversity. Gaga's ambition, persistence, and resilience helped forge her most authentic self, and she unabashedly challenges millions to be their most authentic selves, too.

The Navigational Challenges

The reality is that media professions represent a dynamic, unpredictable journey for most. Successful professionals rarely, if ever, make it "overnight" or "just happen" to be in the right place at the right time. Young and aspiring professionals, in particular, embark on a road that is uncertain and not clearly defined. The road's lack of clarity causes some to give up. Some, I believe, give up not because they lack passion or talent but because they don't have the tools—or a properly loaded suitcase—that equips them for the journey ahead. Although there are as many paths (stories) as there are people who have taken them, several commonalities characterize most media careers. Let's look a bit deeper at these common "navigational" challenges.

The path is often nonlinear (sharp curves). Media professions are not like nursing, accounting, and engineering. People who prepare for such fields have a strong idea of what they are going to do, even if some practices within the professions change over time. The pathway is much different for the media and creative professions. Some may enter or study for the profession with an idea of what they seek to do, but few start there. Typically, a person will hold several jobs both inside and outside the industry, sometimes in positions that are associated with the interest area, sometimes not. Because competition is high and "getting in" is often difficult, many try to get "a" job associated with the industry with the idea of moving to an area that is a better fit to the individual's interests and aspirations. It is not uncommon for a professional to hold half-dozen positions or more in a short time frame. Moreover, a growing number of jobs are "project-based" (e.g., freelance), meaning that individuals are hired for a specific project with no prospects of full-time employment. This "job hopping" will likely take new professionals in a number of directions along the way, some fruitful and some not. Because of this, media professionals are increasingly entrepreneurial in orientation, working to build a personal brand and reputation that enables consistent work. These early "peripheral" jobs may also open doors to opportunities in areas that were previously unconsidered, and additional interests and aptitudes may be developed through interaction with these "new" areas.

Broad array of possibilities (many roads to take). Characteristic of a nonlinear path is a wide range of choices. Both within and across the media and creative industries, the directions one can go seem infinite in terms of locations (LA, New York, Nashville, Austin, and hundreds of cities/towns in between); the types of companies to work with (studio, corporate, independent, local); and the types of jobs available within film, television, music, digital, and publishing. Degrees in communication and media produce among the lowest return on tuition investment among all fields/disciplines.[1] This is partially due to the reality that careers falling under the broad umbrella of "Communication" carry far fewer known or established pathways and consistently reconfigure themselves. Moreover, the media and creative industries increasingly overlap and cross-pollinate. Creation of, and demand for, technology leads to new companies—if not industries—and opportunities. In a mostly collaborative field, with so many possible directions to go in and across industries, from development to sales and marketing, to producing and directing, to cinematography and sound, to recording and artist management, to acting and casting, to being in front of the camera or behind it, there is an almost countless array of leadership and support positions. Although this abundance of possibility and opportunity might be viewed as a positive, the broad range of choices can present an unwieldy navigational challenge.

Highly unpredictable (unknown and newly built roads). The media and creative industries are businesses that inherently rely on technology and audience/buyer approval, which means that the production, distribution, and reception of products are "fluid" and in constant evolution. Business practices often change rapidly with the advent of a new technology or development of a new creative form (or formula). Media professionals must be adaptable in order to navigate changes in current practices and/or stand at the forefront of entirely new industries that are yet unseen. An interesting challenge for aspiring professionals (and media educators) is how to prepare yourself (or others) for industries that don't exist today but will five, ten, and twenty years from now. For example, freshmen who entered college in 1994 could not be prepared through curricula for the Internet explosion when they graduated in 1998 or 1999. Curricula existing in 2008 could not capture the explosion of social media and its impact on the content and marketing of created products. COVID-19 demanded businesses run via remote work, completely altering how business is conducted. How do media professionals best "equip" themselves for these unknowns? Professionals must recognize the fluidity that characterizes industries so dependent on technology and evolving forms of delivery and audience/buyer response.

Extremely competitive (rocky, uphill, thick brush). Despite the broad array of possible careers, media professions remain highly competitive with far more people looking to gain entry than positions available. This is followed by increasingly stiff competition for the most coveted jobs. Enrollments in media programs (e.g., "mass communication," "media arts," and "journalism") continue to be robust, creating high competition, which contributes to the low return on tuition investment for degrees in "Communication" (which includes media). I often tell parents of prospective students that there will be no "job fairs" for the media industries, and some research even shows a *negative* relationship between success and dependence on career placement services in the media industries.[2] Media companies simply do not set up a table to take applications for a producer, director, news anchor/reporter, or writer, not to mention camera operator, recording engineer, grip, editor, or young production assistant (PA). This almost never happens because media businesses have an abundant number of people flock to them (a key reason that individuals make a lower wage, especially early in the career). Those who gain entry usually do so in a "messier" way—as volunteers, through internships, as PAs, in the proverbial "mailroom," taking on multiple responsibilities at a small-market TV station, or as the catch-all "gopher" or "runner" at a sporting event. Some, increasingly, initiate their own content-based businesses, fighting through the thickets of competition to reach ears and eyeballs, hoping to "monetize" these efforts to sustain a livelihood.

If we take a closer look, we see that these uncertainties create obstacles or challenges that often impede both entry and advancement through the media industries. For a young professional, the combination of low pay, lack of encouragement, uninspiring work, and incompatibility with true interests creates an uphill battle to say the least. It takes a special person to not only survive this likely reality but also *thrive* within it. Those who aspire to make feature films, to produce and mix music, to be a journalist, to create and produce video/TV content, or to work in the vast array of professional positions associated with these industries may have different jobs that require different skills, but they usually face a commonly uncommon path, one that is extremely competitive, highly uncertain, very unpredictable, and sometimes unfair.

The reality is that many talented people never see the light of day, and some who are less talented (or even less-than-talented) enjoy success that is perplexing, discouraging, and *infuriating*. More than just "intelligence" or "talent" or technical skills or even "dumb luck," a deeper set of qualities or attributes seems to be at play, distinguishing those who thrive in leading successful lives in the media and creative industries from those who do not attain success or even lose the desire to pursue their dreams.

If a career in the media professions is so difficult and challenging, why would anyone want to do it? A good way to answer this question is to reverse the question into a common cliché: "If it were easy, everyone would do it" is a powerfully instructive term for this book. The opportunity to be involved in highly public professions holds great attraction for many who seek to work within them. More important, the level of challenge, volatility, and risk faced by those who aspire to work in these industries implies that something more is needed to navigate these roads effectively.

The Power of Attributes

You don't have to attain the professional and public successes of Jerry Seinfeld, Oprah Winfrey, Quentin Tarantino, or Lady Gaga to be considered "extraordinary" in media-related professions. However, their successes, along with lesser-known, yet equally extraordinary people, leave behind powerfully instructive clues that you can take and apply to your own career. I do not believe that Oprah Winfrey is *Oprah* or Jerry Seinfeld is *Seinfeld* because they are innately intelligent or talented. Instead, extraordinary media professionals develop a set of attributes that put them into position to access their various talents to full potential. *Seinfeld* might have been a show about "nothing," but it required special qualities to make *Seinfeld* (the person and the series) happen. The "genius" is the attributes they bring to bear.

I use the term *attribute* to describe a set of interrelated qualities or characteristics that are important to achieve extraordinary professional success. Through formal interviews and informal discussions, research as a scholar and observations as a teacher, and experience as the director of programs located in LA and sponsored by the National Association of Broadcasters, I see certain attributes consistently emerge as "important" determinants of *long-term success and growth* in media-related professions. The significance of attributes is that they serve to *drive* the acquisition of talents and skills/knowledge (specific information for a specific job/profession) needed to enter, advance, and, ultimately, achieve extraordinary things.

For example, an individual with a "passion" for something (i.e., an intense love or desire) is going to be driven to learn and retain the specific skills and gain requisite knowledge necessary to earn entry into the area of interest. Contrast this with the person who may be intelligent but is not passionate. Will this person be motivated to fight through the thicket of competition and uncertainties likely to stand in the way? Stated another way, visualize the *dis*passionate media professional. In any media or creative industry, will this person be motivated to develop the hard and soft skills necessary to navigate effectively through these industries? Will this person attract employment opportunities over time?

A closer look at Jerry Seinfeld and Orny Adams from *Comedian* provides a far deeper, more illuminating demonstration of why important attributes enable some to become successful in these challenging professions, while others labor in obscurity or give up altogether. The contrast between these two individuals couldn't be more striking. During the course of the documentary, we see that Orny is struggling; is obsessed with becoming a celebrity; is constantly unhappy, jealous, cocky, and arrogant with no justification; has little respect for the audience paying to see him; is quick to blame, unwilling to accept criticism, and unwilling to take responsibility. Orny seeks to leap past the process necessary to fully develop his talent.

Jerry, by contrast, is guided by *values* that are the by-product of his attributes. Having finished work on one of the most beloved and critically acclaimed comedy series in the history of television (with mounds of money still rolling in through syndication), Jerry went back to what he believes is his true calling, stand-up comedy. With literally hundreds of millions of dollars in the bank, Jerry would never have to work another day in this or several lifetimes. His place in media history and popular culture is fully cemented. His show is an "evergreen" that will never go away.

Yet Jerry was never "married" to *Seinfeld*, and this was why he was able to walk away from the show at the height of its popularity. As *Comedian* chronicles, Jerry also "put to rest" all of his previous stand-up material and started from scratch. Financially, he certainly didn't need to do this. But, internally, for reasons only he needed to understand, Jerry *had* to start again. How many people who experience such extraordinary success would have the motivation to do this? Money isn't the core reason Jerry Seinfeld does what he does, and that's exactly why he has so much of it.

So, why is Jerry Seinfeld "Jerry Seinfeld"? In reference to my favorite episode of *Seinfeld*, Jerry is the exact opposite of Orny Adams. He is adaptable, respects the audience, and seeks to challenge himself in a variety of venues, not just where it's safe. Jerry also knows who he is and has the courage to fail in front of an audience, which he painfully does on several occasions as he develops material. (Facing the danger of not being funny *is* dangerous!) Even though money is not an issue for Jerry, he has a lot to lose by not being funny because his well-earned reputation could be damaged. He sets high standards for himself, is hard on himself, but is driven to prove that he still has it. He has a vision of where he wants to get to—one hour of funny material—and this pulls him forward toward his goals. He pays attention to what is working and what is not working. As a rare established comedian who is starting over (almost), he's willing to go through the process to get back to where he wants to be.

Late in *Comedian*, an introspective Jerry Seinfeld says, "I just want to do what I love to do. . . . I want to explore this thing. That's what I keep thinking: There's something else out there. I just feel like I can go somewhere with it—I don't know where." For me, these words are quite inspiring, especially coming from someone who has already achieved more than most of us could dream to achieve.

Is Jerry more *innately* intelligent or talented than Orny? Perhaps. Or has Jerry Seinfeld consciously and subconsciously developed an array of compelling attributes that have propelled him to reach extraordinary heights? If so, what can we learn from him, other high achievers, and successful up-and-comers in a range of media professions to provide better distinctions for those who seek to develop successful careers? Regardless of the specific industry, achievement in the media industries usually requires more than having a marketable skill and knowledge. Plenty of people have innate ability and a high intelligence quotient (IQ). These qualities, while potentially important, are rarely enough without key attributes to drive them. Within industries this challenging, competitive, evolving, unpredictable, and risky, an additional dimension is necessary to put one into position to achieve extraordinary things.

The triangulation of attributes with skills and knowledge is a vital link in the chain for the extraordinary media professional. Application of key personality (and personal) attributes helps to complete the fully loaded suitcase for you to survive in the early stages of a career and thrive long term in these industries. These compelling attributes will help distinguish you from the "average" media professional (or, in many cases, the *former* media professional). Your *real* "talent" may be your ability to develop the attributes that enable you to succeed in an uncertain, ever-evolving, highly competitive set of industries.

This book represents the first attempt to describe and illustrate the attributes that lead to long-term success in the media industries. Heightened development of the attributes will increase your ability to navigate through the thickets, hills, newly built roads, and sharp curves that ultimately help make you an extraordinary professional. In the process, this book seeks to help you connect your personal values with what you want to do within these professions *and* provides practical help along the way. The journey to distinction represents a race without a true finish line in dynamic, evolving industries and is significantly aided by the attributes you bring to bear.

I hope you are excited by this challenge!

A Model for Extraordinary Media Professionals

Attribute[1]: A property, quality or feature belonging to or representative of a person or thing

Extraordinary: Beyond what is ordinary or usual; highly exceptional, remarkable

Unlike most college freshmen finishing up his first year, Matthew Rhodes didn't return home to work a summer job. Instead, he boarded a Greyhound bus near Cleveland with a suitcase and $800 in his pocket and headed to LA. Matt had *zero* contacts in Hollywood, no residence to go to, and no internship lined up.

What he did "have" was a burning, nearly obsessive, desire to work in movies.

With no concrete knowledge of what to do or where to go, Matt went to Paramount, a major motion picture studio, and was promptly stopped at the security gate. He tried to talk his way in. Access denied.

For the next several days, Matt sneaked on the Paramount lot through various entrances, walking on with groups checking in for work or attending a show taping. Once inside, Matt walked into offices and bungalows asking anyone and everyone for an internship. Each day security eventually found him and kicked him out. Finally, a security guard told Matt to never come back to Paramount or he would be arrested.

Young with almost no money, Matt couldn't afford to get arrested.

But the security guard took notice, if warily.

"Man, you sure are persistent," the guard told Matt. Then, pointing south to a building on the other side of Melrose Avenue, the security guard said, "Go across the street and try there. Maybe they'll help you out."

Across the street was Raleigh Studios, a much smaller production facility with relatively less security (this was pre-9/11) and a less corporate-y vibe.

Sure enough, getting into Raleigh was easy. Probably too easy. The security guard at Raleigh simply waved at Matt and let him through the gate.

Indeed, Raleigh was a lot different. Matt walked around the entire lot, which felt like a ghost town compared to Paramount. Every office and bungalow was empty, as were the soundstages.

Except for Stage 11. Something was obviously going on there. Several large trucks were outside the stage with people going in and out. Matt walked in through the stage door, where he saw the hustle-bustle of a film set: PAs, grips, sound techs, and other personnel walking briskly to perform tasks unknown. Matt tried to blend in, careful not to draw too much attention to how he got there.

Matt hung around the set of *Single White Female*, and after a couple of days, the production manager asked Matt who he was. Matt gave him his speech about looking for an internship.

"For free?" the production manager asked.

"Yes."

"You're hired."

For the rest of that summer, Matt showed up at Raleigh Studios to work as a PA. No pay. No internship credit. No problem. Matt was thrilled to be there.

Soon enough, Matt began to strike up conversations with producers and crew, who came to know of Matt as a reliable presence that would do any task, "big or small." Matt listened carefully. He observed the process and how people interacted. He asked questions but was careful not to get in anyone's way.

Following a summer of working on a movie, Matt returned to Ohio to continue college. Along with a really cool experience and expanded knowledge of how a film production worked, Matt brought back something equally valuable: dozens of contacts who would continue to work in films and would not soon forget the "scrappy kid from Ohio" who walked onto a movie set and showed an unrelenting work ethic and an eagerness to learn.

Each summer after that, Matt returned to LA. Through contacts from that first summer, Matt worked on various productions and interned at a major talent agency following a recommendation from a producer who was impressed with Matt's focus and drive.

Matt's experience at the talent agency eventually led him to Scott Rudin, one of the most successful producers in Hollywood history. Rudin was (and is) notorious for being one of the most demanding, sometimes demeaning, bosses in this or any industry. None of Rudin's previous assistants had ever lasted a year; many lasted far less than that.

It wasn't easy, to say the least. Matt was essentially on call 24/7 and, at times, endured rough treatment, none of which he or anyone should endure. Having his hand stapled by Scott Rudin and being pushed out of a moving car are just two of the indignities Matt endured. The film *Swimming with Sharks* is loosely based on Scott Rudin. Check it out. Matt stuck it out.

Due to Rudin's prolific *and* "difficult" status, Matt soon gained a reputation in Hollywood circles for his thick skin, work ethic, fearlessness, and extreme competence. People were amazed that he had stuck it out with Scott Rudin. For *two years*.

Finally, Matt, too, was fired. But he had gained credibility and learned so much about producing. He felt ready, at age twenty-seven, to start his own production company. The name of his new company: Persistent Entertainment.

Ten years and more than two dozen films later, Matt Rhodes had become known for, among other things, his special skill of selling international rights to films to ensure their profitability (before ever reaching theatrical release).

One day he was invited to the home of Peter Guber, another legendary producer and then-chairman of Mandalay Entertainment. After a two-hour meeting, Guber offered Matt the position of president of Mandalay Vision, the company's motion picture arm. Three years later, Matt moved on to be president of production at Bold Films, which produced several critically acclaimed and commercially successful movies (such as *Whiplash*).

Matt Rhodes's (or Matt's *road* to) success story, which started on a Greyhound with a few hundred dollars in his pocket, is singular in detail, yet strikingly common for extraordinary media professionals. No two stories are exactly alike. Yet, almost without exception, the story of success is about more than innate talent or a "hard" skill. Important additional attributes help fuel successful people in the media industries.

What will be *your* road to success?

The 12 Attributes Model

The 12 Attributes introduced next—and detailed in subsequent chapters—represent a "model of attributes" to illustrate *extraordinary* media professionals. Individually, each attribute is important to media-related professions. Collectively, the 12 Attributes, functioning as an integrated *system* of attributes, generates synergistic levels of understanding and momentum toward long-term success in media professions. Moreover, the attributes described here are *dynamic* in that they offer no true end point. Personal and professional development is approached as a never-ending endeavor, because as your attributes and skills continue to develop, you will be in position to enjoy exciting new challenges that will further enhance the power of these key attributes.

Distilled to its essence, the media professions seek smart-working, motivated, passionate, well-rounded, solution-oriented people who are adaptable, reliable, eager to learn and grow, and enjoyable to be around. These individuals do what it takes, within correct principles, to successfully get the job—big or small—done. The *extraordinary* professional gains access to people and resources to achieve and contribute at levels greater than the sum of the individual attributes. This builds confidence and a certain "toughness" that in turn leads to enhanced (and/or refined) access to people, resources, and opportunities. The model provided (see figure 1) visually represents the attributes and how various elements are connected. These are organized into "arenas of attributes" labeled "Big Picture," "Active," "Enduring," and "Reinforcing." The sections below introduce each attribute and illustrate how they work and interconnect.

The Big Picture Attributes

The Big Picture starts with *YOU* and is built on connecting who you are to your Passion(s); your ongoing thirst to achieve (Ambition); and your ability to *connect* effectively with people in your professional network. Big Picture attributes are foundational characteristics that guide your overall approach to career choice and professional development.

12 Attributes of Extraordinary Media Professionals

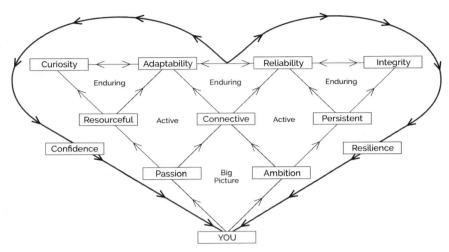

Figure 1

Of all of the important attributes to be described, *YOU* remain the most critical, instigating element in the professional (and personal) development equation. Just as attaining a strike in bowling is next to impossible without hitting the headpin, success in the highly competitive, uncertain media industries starts with the unique attributes that you bring to any and every situation. Understanding who you are, what you are good at/interested in, and why you seek to pursue a career in media professions is of utmost relevance. What makes you an interesting person? What is unique about you? What key events or defining moments (DMs) helped form your values and led you to a belief that a career in media or creative professions should be your career (and life) choice? What skills or aptitudes seem to come "naturally" to you? Your authentic personal qualities, plus the talents and skills you bring, are critical elements for your own development and career success. Moreover, it's critical to *accurately* understand who you are and how your unique "talents" connect to your own values and aspirations.

Passion represents a key "prerequisite" in The Big Picture to attain extraordinary success in media professions. Across the various industries—film, television, recording, digital, publishing, and all associated fields—"having a passion" is an often-cited quality or attribute by highly successful media professionals. Success and achievement in the competitive, uncertain media industries is exceedingly difficult without having an emotionally driven desire (or *love*) for this work. Thus, passion is not merely about "wanting to" work in some area of the media industries but represents the *having to* within the individual. It is an internalized value that is central, fundamental, and essential to develop other key attributes necessary to be "extraordinary" in media-related professions. Someone with a passion for something carries an emotional attachment to whatever and whoever they are passionate toward, and thus is willing to do more than someone who is not as emotionally invested. One's specific passion may shift or change altogether during the course of a career, but passion remains an essential element to extraordinary long-term success.

Although passion is highly important, it's often not enough to achieve success. For example, I can have a passion for (or "love") movies, but this isn't sufficient to develop a successful *career* in the movie industry. *Ambition* represents an essential "want to" in The Big Picture. Ambitious media professionals "dream big" and have the drive to make those dreams a reality. Media professions are heavily populated with strivers. Ambitious media professionals use their imaginations to craft a compelling future and then take concrete steps to reach their aspirations.

Connective completes the diamond of Big Picture attributes and also represents the *central nervous system* for the entire attributes model, because the ability to connect "radiates" to other attributes. The importance of this attribute cannot be overstated, and the extraordinary media professional recognizes how important meaningful relationships are when working in people- and audience/user-driven industries. An individual that connects with high effectiveness can open doors of opportunity far more powerful than a strong resume or display of talent. Media professionals must work with one another, often in high-pressure, long-day environments, and the ability to build strong bonds with peers and colleagues is critical to long-term success.

The Active Attributes

The Big Picture attributes are critical, but not sufficient, for success. They are manifest through *quality action*. The next three attributes—Resourceful, Connective, and Persistent—represent core active attributes as a result of your effective orientation to The Big Picture. The Active Attributes bring your passions and ambitions to life, allowing you to "activate" knowledge, skills, and talents to a high level, which enables professional opportunity while also promoting personal and professional development. Your passion for a career in the media industries is enhanced by the desire to resourcefully "figure it out." But more than that, resourceful people, fueled by their passions, are creative problem-solvers (i.e., solution-oriented) with the ability to act imaginatively toward personal, creative, and organizational ends. Your ambition to succeed is fueled by your willingness to persistently "stick it out" when met by inevitable obstacles or challenges when you dare to "dream big." Together, the ability to "figure it out" (Resourceful) and "stick it out" (Persistent) are critical to build leverage and advance in the media professions.

The orientation to persist through challenging goals and to resourcefully problem-solve offer limited value if you're unable to "connect" these efforts with people and organizations. Thus, Connective is a central fiber among the active attributes—and the entire model—and carries significant power for the aspiring or current media professional. The collaborative, often project-based, industries require "who you know" and "who knows you" to a degree that surpasses almost any other profession. As an active attribute, strong connections are built via hard and *smart* work, and the willingness to "put yourself out there" to create relationships in (and out of) the industry. The ability to connect effectively can also lead to direct career opportunities, whether it's selling a script idea, being "pulled into" a new project, or convincing people to invest money in your idea. Persistent individuals, fueled by their ambitions, connect with professionals who are also "in it to win." Resourceful professionals, activated by passion, build connections through positive energy and a solution orientation.

The Enduring Attributes

The ability to make meaningful connections, to act with imagination, and to persist toward goals leads to a third set of attributes to complete the "ten-pin strike" for extraordinary media professionals. The Enduring Attributes—Curiosity, Adaptability, Reliability, and Integrity—represent attributes that help sustain attributes developed in The Big Picture and through active application. These four attributes are important as you embark on a career and also foster long-term relevance within the media professions.

The thirst to continually learn and grow (Curiosity); the ability to adapt to gradual or sudden changes/demands in work or industry environments (Adaptability); being a consistent and trustworthy "go-to" person (Reliability); and having a reputation as ethical and principled (Integrity) are all critical to a successful long-term career in the media and creative industries. As the model shows, Adaptability completes an "active diamond" that includes Passion, Resourceful, and Connective, while Reliability completes an "active diamond" of Ambition, Persistent, and Connective. Adaptability and Reliability hold this more central presence because media professionals rate these two attributes as the *most important* toward career success.[2] Please also note that Connective is *connected* to the critical attributes of Adaptability and Reliability. Those who can adapt most readily to changing situations and can be consistently "counted on" will naturally connect with key people and will build a positive reputation in the process.

Ongoing interest about people, stories, industry trends, processes, and/or technology breeds a special type of IQ called InQuisitiveness. People who display genuine curiosity actively, *organically*, seek to learn and grow, are interested in how things "work," ask questions, and make important connections (both conceptually and with people) that benefit everyone involved. Simply put, those with a broad knowledge base have "multiple lenses/perspectives" to draw from, are better-able to develop solutions, and adapt more effectively to changes. The result of having curiosity is the ability, orientation, and inclination to *grow* over the long term.

Integrity is the moral foundation through which you make decisions, how you treat people, and how you respond to challenges. Media professionals soon discover how shockingly small this world is, and your integrity impacts your reputation, your reliability, and how you respond when challenged to uphold your principles in the face of adversity. Those with integrity can be relied upon to act ethically and treat people with respect, even when it's not expedient to do so. Media professionals with integrity can "sleep well at night" and also gain opportunities over time due to a positive reputation.

The Reinforcing Attributes

Development of the various Big Picture, Active, and Enduring attributes—individually and in tandem—are reinforcing and encourage continual pursuit of career goals, new opportunities, and personal development. These arrows point back to YOU as they offer clarifying self-distinctions about who you are (as you continue to grow personally and professionally), which additionally reinforces Big Picture, Active, and Enduring attributes needed to enhance your personal and professional successes over the long term.

Confidence is a product of *earned* self-assuredness as a result of the attributes and the specific talents you develop. Confident media professionals believe in their abilities and are "freed" to accomplish whatever they set out to do. You are more inclined to take risks and be undeterred by temporary setbacks. Your earned confidence will naturally attract more opportunities through your growing relationship network.

Resilience "toughens you up" so that your capacity to handle adversity and challenges expands. In the process—and more important—you'll gain greater insight into who you are and what *really* matters to you. The phrase "What doesn't kill you makes you stronger" is an overstatement in the technical sense and yet carries a profound truth that helps many media professionals thrive in the industry. As American author Carol Orsborn states, "Mastering the art of resilience does much more than restore you to who you once thought you were. Rather, you emerge from the experience transformed into a truer expression of who you were really meant to be."[3]

Getting to the *Heart* of the Matter

A wonderful surprise happened when I first penciled out a visual model of the important attributes: the reinforcing lines from the top of the model back to the point "YOU" formed a heart shape! This seemed to be a perfect encapsulation of the model and a metaphor for the process of developing a successful career in the media professions. I believe the most extraordinary media professionals work from the heart. The many definitions of "heart" further capture—and *reinforce*—the multitude of attributes that are necessary to survive and *thrive* long term in media-related professions, while also representing the life-giving, life-enhancing nature of "heart" for exceptional professionals. Here are some definitions of "heart":

The vital center and source of one's being, emotions, and sensibilities;
The repository of one's deepest and sincerest feelings and beliefs;
The seat of intellect or imagination;
The most important or essential part;
Courage, resolution, fortitude;
The firmness of will or the callousness required to carry out an unpleasant task or responsibility;
Completely, entirely (as with "all one's heart");

With great willingness or pleasure;
The courage to carry on;
The choicest or most essential or most vital part of some idea or experience.

Wow. "Heart," in its various iterations, *is* the extraordinary media professional!

Impact of Developing the 12 Attributes

The model's combination of Big Picture, Active, Enduring, and Reinforcing attributes reflects a continuous, never-ending progression toward personal development and greater distinction in the media professions. It visualizes how attributes might work as a *system* to produce extraordinary results over time. In other words, your successful career is made possible by you, enabled by your passion, ambition, and ability to connect; activated with resourcefulness, persistence, and connections you make; endures with curiosity, adaptability, reliability, and integrity; and is then reinforced through confidence and resilience.

With these attributes in your suitcase you are able to develop the important skills relevant to your career and also navigate through the uncertain paths with optimal effectiveness. The road, at times, will continue to be uphill, rocky, and winding, but you'll be better equipped to handle the challenges and difficulties ahead. You will be enterprising and industrious, motivated and energetic, and optimally equipped to thrive in media-related professions over time. You will come to appreciate, even enjoy, the process of growth that your career demands. Internalization of these attributes will help make young and aspiring professionals "feel" successful (even if the financial rewards trail initially) and will keep more experienced, accomplished professionals motivated to seek greater personal and professional distinction.

The model is intended to be dynamic, because your own values will shift and change to some degree during the course of your life and career. As you age, reaching different stages in your career (e.g., assuming more responsibilities and leadership roles) and life (e.g., marriage and family), your priorities and what's important to you will shift and evolve. Be ready for this and embrace it. In reality, extraordinary media professionals are in a continual state of growth and development throughout their careers, consistently seeking new, meaningful challenges along the way.

The product of this ongoing process is a sum greater than the individual parts, analogous to the sport of bowling. Certainly, knocking down eight pins (or attributes) will provide a better "score" than knocking down six pins. But the product of attaining ten attributes carries synergistic benefits similar to knocking down all ten pins. With a strike, you are able to count your next two rolls (the Reinforcing Attributes, if you will) onto the previous score. Thus, a score of six in all ten frames gives you a score of sixty, but a score of ten with each roll produces a score not of 100 but *300!* Similarly, a "strike of attributes" significantly increases your ongoing performance and development, which in turn enables higher levels of mastery and achievement. This seems to be a useful approach to conceptualize both the process and momentum-based effects of *continually* developing the 12 Attributes throughout your career.

Yet, as with bowling, the pins might not fall the same way for each person. A perfect game in bowling is rare and difficult to achieve. It takes great skill—and a little luck—during the process. Pitchers in baseball, to use another analogy, who have been fortunate enough to throw a perfect game are almost always "saved" by a spectacular defensive play or feel "lucky" when a hitter misses a "fat" pitch. This is a way of stating that attributes are not manifest equally in all of us. Some attributes described in this book may seem to be a "natural" part of you—and perhaps a core part of what defines *YOU*—while other attributes may be less developed or new concepts altogether. The key is to realize that we are blessed with the ability to stand outside ourselves and consciously work to internalize and activate—or at least *improve*—attributes we want/need and to eliminate those that are self-limiting.

In essence, you are both the headpin *and* the ball itself. How you spin the ball as you strike the pins is a critical part of the equation. Bowling experts explain that you cannot achieve maximum results by hitting the headpin squarely in the middle with no spin. You give yourself a "chance" for a strike, but over time you will not maximize your results without angle and spin. The angle represents what's uniquely "you" and the spin represents the amount of energy you bring. You control the ball, how it spins, and these key attributes will help lead you to extraordinary heights.

A key benefit of the model is that these important attributes will remain constant, true, and timeless, even as technology, distribution, media and communication forms, and creative and business practices inevitably evolve and/or change altogether. For example, the need to have "passion" will exist today and tomorrow in the media industries, even as the passion may be directed toward new, evolving forms. The value of developing important connections within and across media organizations will remain constant, even as the modes of communication change. These attributes will remain meaningful five, ten, twenty, or even fifty years from now—throughout your life and career. The intent is for you to be able to see yourself in these attributes, regardless of your experience level.

And while I believe the attributes described here are important or "good" for almost any vocation, few *require* the activation of such a broad array of attributes as do the media industries. The professions are extremely competitive; ego-, story-, and technology-driven; always evolving; highly collaborative; and very unpredictable. Those who make it through this minefield—and even make the minefield work *for* them—reach the other side with great satisfaction because they accessed the important attributes that helped drive the successes. These same professionals never become complacent because the very attributes that helped fuel the successes also help *liberate* successful people to reach even greater heights. This is my definition of the extraordinary media professional, and my greatest desire for you moving forward.

How to *Use* This Book

Early in the process of developing this book, I would ask media professionals questions about success in terms of "qualities" rather than attributes (i.e., what *qualities* does someone need to be successful in the media/creative industries?). As I reflected on this question, I came to believe that "qualities" imply something inherent or innate, while attributes represent characteristics that can be developed. Although this distinction may be more semantic than real, it is the perspective of this book that each attribute can, indeed, be developed and enriched through awareness, understanding, motivation, and application. Just as one's internal values may shift due to experiences and maturity, so, too, can attributes be developed through self-awareness and effective application.

Thus, this book is intended to be *used*, not merely "read." The chapters that follow will expand on the importance of the 12 Attributes by providing descriptions and illustrations of how they function for media professionals at all experience levels. Each attribute will include "Attribute Tips for Career Success," which will offer practical suggestions to help benefit your career, and additional "sidebars" of insights relevant to the attribute. Each attribute chapter will conclude with exercises to help you further develop the attribute. I urge you to *use* these ideas and exercises toward your own personal and professional development. Be honest with yourself. Read this with both self-reflection and a desire to develop these attributes to the best of your ability. Don't wait to master one attribute before proceeding to another, because the model is designed as an *interconnection* of attributes and encourages simultaneous development of these important concepts.

As you continue, it is important to emphasize that there are many definitions of success. The extraordinarily successful media professional might lead a major film studio or serve the community at a local TV station or production company. Your aspirations should be *your* aspirations, in congruence with who you are and your own deepest values. That's why the model starts with *YOU*. The focus should be on what you want to do, where you want to do it, and a deep understanding of *why* you are driven toward these professions. Hopefully, this book will help put you in touch with these elements so that you are moving in concert with your own personal values and aspirations. This, however, must be *self*-determined: this book is not offered to illustrate *what* you should do, but rather your approach to *why* and *how* you go about developing your career in media in a successful way.

However, development of these attributes should naturally lead you to be open to new opportunities, possibilities, and challenges in connection with your personal and professional values. Your definition of success may change as you experience the profession and/or encounter life-changing shifts. Regardless, mastery of the attributes won't make your road to success "easy." Your pathway into and up the media professions will remain, at times, challenging. But I believe they will help you do what it takes to build a successful career within correct principles. I hope you will benefit from this conceptualization of career success and *use* the attributes that follow on your road to success.

Part I

The Big Picture

A Broad Overview or Perspective

Don't aim at success—the more you aim at it and make it a target, the more you are going to miss it. *For success, like happiness, cannot be pursued; it must ensue,* and it does so as the unintended side-effect of one's dedication to a cause greater than oneself or as the by-product of one's surrender to a person other than oneself. Happiness must happen, and the same holds for success: you have to let it happen by not caring about it. I want you to listen to what your conscience commands you to do and go on to carry it out to the best of your knowledge. Then you will live to see that in the long run—in the long run, I say!—success will follow you precisely because you had forgotten to think about it.[1]

—Viktor E. Frankl

The above quote from Viktor Frankl, a renowned psychiatrist who survived Nazi concentration camps and went on to write one of the most influential books ever about the human condition, is one I've spent hours thinking about. So much focus in our culture is about "being happy." Google that phrase and you'll find endless articles about happiness (or how to avoid unhappiness). It's no wonder. The "*Pursuit* of Happiness" is literally embedded in the U.S. Constitution. And yet, year in and year out, only about one-third of adults consider themselves happy, about two-thirds do not "like" their jobs,[2] and people striving to achieve our common cultural definitions of "success" (money, title) rarely seem to find real satisfaction as a result of these pursuits.

A key assumption of this book is that you're aspiring to build a successful, *long-lasting* career and you do not view media and creative professions as simply "a job." There is something intrinsically fascinating and intriguing about being involved in the process of *creating content* and directing those expressions toward a larger public and culture. You want to *affect* people through your connection to ideas, stories, and processes. As the late Robin Williams once said, "No matter what people tell you, your words and ideas can change the world." These *pursuits* are "side effects" and "by-products" of who you genuinely are, what you're inspired to do, and your own internal, *self-determined* motivations to make an impact in collaboration with others.

The Big Picture is not simply about your "career" in the media professions (or any profession) but about how you want to live and approach your life, of which your work life can be one intrinsic part. Your passions and ambitions should be by-products of who you are and how you connect with others along with attributes that activate and enable your long-term successes, whatever they are and however they manifest themselves.

"Passion and ambition. Once you lose those two things, stop," says filmmaker Reena Dutt. "If you don't have ambition or passion, you're probably not going to be full of joy either. Life's too short."

This is The Big Picture, and the media/creative professions offer one of the most compelling, dynamic means toward actualizing who you really are.

Success, like happiness, is not a pursuit; it ensues . . .

YOU

The nature or character of the person addressed

When you have a career, there's never enough time. When you have a job, there's too much time.

—Chris Rock

My dad was a master psychologist. Not in any formal, trained way, but in the ways of life and motivating influences. During the summer before I started college, he secured a job for me at a factory in Wynne, Arkansas. My job for eight hours each and every day: putting six-foot rubber tubes into a box and shoving the box down a conveyer belt. I didn't know what the rubber tubes were used for and, importantly, *didn't care*. The job was not particularly difficult, but it was *incredibly boring*. To say that I was uninterested in this job would be a colossal understatement.

I soon realized that I could never do this for a living eight hours a day, forty hours a week. There was nothing "wrong" with the job or vocation (and I made much more money that summer than I ever had). I enjoyed the people I worked with but knew I wouldn't be fulfilled or interested doing such monotonous work. Yet, to this day, I point to that experience as perhaps the most important job I ever had, because it provided a clear distinction about the type of work I *didn't* want to do while providing great insight into who *I* am. My dad knew exactly what he was doing. If I had any inclination about not going to college or not working hard enough to stay in school, this experience made it compellingly clear.

A similar example has probably happened to you, either in an uninspiring job unrelated to the media professions or perhaps in a media-specific internship or job. You learned key insights about what you *don't* want to do, while learning something important about who you are, which led to distinctions or reinforcements toward the things you want to do and the types of pursuits that might ensue.

Thousands of successful media professionals are doing something very different from their first jobs (thank goodness!), while some others developed a specific interest and followed this toward what they are doing. Most worked at crappy jobs—often with crappy people—along the way. Yet the most successful media professionals remain motivated and passionate, are happy with what ensued, and look back at the struggles with an odd nostalgia, even gratitude, that the early experiences happened as they did. Regardless of the pathways you take, these "successes" will be the by-product, in The Big Picture, of connecting your own unique talents with your passions, ambitions, and people who create opportunities to grow and advance.

The Accurate You

Randall Winston, a producer for the classic TV series *Scrubs* (among many others), was once asked by an aspiring media professional, "What advice would you give about preparing for a career?"

"What do you want to do?" Randall asked.

"Be a writer," the student said.

"Write," Randall responded.

The student, thinking Randall misunderstood the answer, said, "Yes, a writer."

"Write," Randall responded again. "If you're a writer, you should be writing."

(Okay, not exactly on the level of Abbott and Costello's classic "Who's on First?" but I do the best I can with the material I have.)

"Are you?" Randall then added.

"I'm a writing major," the student replied. "I write scripts for class, mostly."

"If you're a writer, then you should be writing when no one else is requiring it."

One of the common pieces of advice provided by successful media and entertainment professionals to young or aspiring professionals is to "know yourself." Why? Because established professionals often see a mismatch between what someone states they "want" to do, what someone is actually "good" at, and what someone is spending their time doing. The media professions are challenging enough as they are, but pulling yourself in directions that are not in concert with your true values and interests makes this challenge all the more difficult. And yet this happens all the time. We are attracted to the allure of what the content industries offer but less mindful of how our values and true interests connect with our aspirations. Scores of talented people go nowhere in the media professions, and others with modest innate talents do extraordinary things. A key reason for this is an inaccurate self-assessment and/or a misguided belief that you need to be someone other than who you are to succeed in these challenging professions.

ATTRIBUTE TIP FOR CAREER SUCCESS

Prepare a Short Personal Pitch

In many job/internship interviews, the first question (which is not technically a question) is "So, tell me about yourself." On the surface, this may seem like an easy, "softball" question and I think it's generally intended as such. Beneath the surface, this is often difficult to answer in a clear, succinct way, and many interviews get off to a less-than-stellar start. You don't want to ramble in your answer. You want to show that you can clearly, confidently, and genuinely articulate the essence of who you are.

And that's the subtext of this "question": How well can you articulate *who you are*? Whether you are actually asked this specific question (or a variation) is ultimately unimportant because your knowledge of the answer will come across through the course of the interaction. More important, the ability to state who you are in any formal or informal encounter is an important skill to execute.

So, prepare a thirty-second (or one-minute) "Personal Statement" that conveys what you want people to know about you. What are your interests? What makes you interes*ting*? Do you have a (very) brief story or anecdote that compellingly illustrates a key insight of who you are? What drew you to your current interests? Why will you be a great person to work with? Given the opportunity to make an impression on someone (in an interview or chance meeting), what would you state about your authentic self to make a compelling/strong impression? (Note: You could also write this down in about 500 words for a written representation, but it's important to practice out loud.) Thirty seconds or a minute is not a lot of time, but you can actually say a lot in this span. The key is to make your words count and to *know* it (not strictly memorize it) so that you can be spontaneous and adapt to any specific encounter.

Always have your short "pitch" at the ready: these opportunities don't only happen during formal interviews but also during unexpected, impromptu encounters. You never know when an opportunity might present itself to make a positive impression. Revisit "your pitch" every three months or so to see if new experiences or self-discoveries prompt recalibration of your pitch.

The 12 Attributes Model starts with YOU because you are both the starting point and the single most important attribute. *You* are the activator of all other attributes in the model, and your unique qualities (which could include skills, knowledge, and other attributes inside and outside the model) help serve to distinguish you and your uniquely individual qualities. Even more important, you are *responsible* for developing and driving the important attributes found in the model, so a focus on you—an accurate self-assessment of your values, talents, and aspirations—is of utmost relevance to your career and how effectively you enact the attributes of extraordinary media professionals.

The media and creative industries value both interested and interes*ting* people who can add value to stories, ideas, concepts, productions, organizations, and markets—and do this via collaboration that may involve a select few and/or hundreds. Those who succeed the most have distinctive personalities along with a strong willingness to work hard *and smart*. Just as the created products generated by the media industries are not shoved down an assembly line like so many rubber tubes going who-knows-where, so, too, are the extraordinary people that populate these professions.

"Who you are is what's going to make your work better," says Herb Trawick, creator and cohost of *Pensado's Place*, a highly successful YouTube series that unexpectedly took Trawick's career in new directions after three decades in the music industry. "What is your personal signature in your work? What makes me hire *you* as opposed to another person? It's something you do that's distinct."

It took Chelsea Peters (Chelsea Stardust professionally), a rising horror film director, eleven years in the industry before she made her first feature film. Along the way, she worked various assistant roles in Hollywood, dealt with bosses both nurturing and mercurial, continued to persevere and connect and, importantly, never forgot who she is and how her aspirations connected to her deeper values. "I've always loved movies for as long as I can remember," Peters says. "I watched movies all the time with my Dad and I saw the AFI 100 (top 100 films of all time as voted by the American Film Institute) before I finished high school.

"Directing is something I've always been drawn to, but it wasn't until I was a little older that I watched the credits of movies and noticed who the directors are. . . . I just love to tell stories; I think filmmaking is the ultimate form of expression. I like being a leader, but with filmmaking it's not just one person: it's a team of people which I think a lot of people forget. I love collaborating. I also realized, if this doesn't work out I'm f—d because there's nothing else I'd rather be doing."

Successful media professionals have a clear idea of who they are and at least a general idea of what they want their careers to be about (even if they, like Trawick, can't always anticipate exactly where life's successes will take them). The process to get wherever "there" is takes time and very rarely happens overnight (actually, *never* happens overnight). But it becomes important to get a good handle on what that "you" is, and to continually pay attention and re-evaluate as you go along. Because the essence of this question involves *you*, you should attack the questions and self-evaluations with energy and *honesty* because you'll continue to grow and develop as part of this process.

YOU-PHEMISMS (CAREER-RELATED CLICHÉS TO TAKE TO HEART)

You can only make a first impression once.
It's who you know and who knows you (for the right reasons).
Younger, less talented people will advance before you (and vice versa).
Your first job(s) will be beneath your education level.
You probably won't have the career you anticipated.
You will get most of your jobs through relationships, not resumes.

Some Key Questions to Ask Yourself

Answer for yourself the following:

What hobbies/interests will you spend hours doing with friends or when no one else is around?
What is your "knack" (i.e., what do you believe you're naturally good at)?
What do you wish you were better at?
What will you exhaustively spend time on that doesn't feel like "work" *to you*?
What do you want to be known for?
What is *your* definition of success?

These are *not* rhetorical questions. Please take out a pad or your computer and *answer each* of the above as honestly, specifically, and completely as you can. Your answers may have no direct connection with media (and that's okay) and can be a great starting point for self-evaluation. They can help lead you toward a *clear* assessment of who you are, what you might bring to the table, and what you're inclined toward pursuing.

What other attributes—perhaps already included in the model or outside the model—do you offer? These could be your sense of humor, your ability to visualize, your optimism, an inclination to obsess about things you care about, your competitiveness, specific talents that you are developing, or several other possibilities. Your values and aspirations will shift, at least to some degree, as you age, gain experience, change jobs, attain more responsibilities, start a family, and so on. You'll continually make these distinctions and should seek to make sure who you are is aligned with what you seek to do and who you seek to be. The passionate, ambitious media professional will work at optimum effectiveness (and efficiency) by being in tune with who they are, tapped into the values and aspirations that will lead to a productive, even extraordinary career.

Take, for example, your "knack." Understanding what you're good at can be incredibly instructive as you're determining your career paths and pursuits in media-related professions. Are you naturally good at connecting with people? Does your sense of humor help you connect easily with people? Do you feel particularly "at home" with technology (or not)? Are you effective working with others or are you equally, perhaps more, comfortable working by yourself? Are you great when diving into the details? Are you a great listener? Do others look to you to help solve problems or resolve conflicts? Do you enjoy writing (or, if not "enjoy," do you do this *on your own*, not solely for a class)? Are you drawn to adventurous, unknown situations? Do you get in food lines *before* they get long (that's *my* knack!)? Notice that none of the aforementioned questions is specific to media professions. But understanding what you're naturally good at (or believe you're naturally good at) offers valuable insights into you and the arenas of work you might seek to pursue. People with each of the aforementioned "knacks" (individually or in combination)—except the last one—have found enormous successes in the media professions.

Of equal importance is a clear understanding of your "weaknesses"—the things you seek to *avoid*, or important attributes you need to improve upon as you pursue specific professions. Again, you must be willing to undertake an *accurate* assessment of these needed areas so that you can improve upon them, partner with people who "fill your gaps" (as your own strengths might help offset their "weaknesses"), or seek jobs that allow you to avoid the most glaring weaknesses. As described in the previous chapter, accurate awareness and personal motivation can help at least improve or mitigate your perceived or real weaknesses. Getting an accurate self-assessment will help lead you in a productive direction.

"The most important thing I've learned is to embrace the talents I have, not the talents I wished I had. When I started doing that, I found success," says writer/producer David Alan Hall.[1] It's important to know your weaknesses while relying on your strengths.

"It's a futile battle to try to change yourself," says Hope Groves, vice president of content technologies at Global Eagle Entertainment. "Instead, know yourself. We all have to do a bit of what we don't like in any career, but to know it is to ensure you can stay motivated and get through it . . . to get to the good stuff."

You and the 10,000-Hour Rule

The well-known "10,000-hour rule" states that an individual must spend a minimum of 10,000 hours on a pursuit to "master" that skill.[2] Consider what 10,000 hours implies: forty hours a week, fifty weeks a year (allowing two weeks of well-earned vacation) for *five* years (or twenty hours a week for *ten* years)! You may be well on your way to achieving this mastery in your area of interest, or you may be and have not consciously considered it. I am not suggesting that you should keep a timesheet of your hours spent on activities of interest to you, but rather that you should be aware of what you're spending your time on (or, perhaps, what you *should* be spending your time on) and what that says about you in pursuit of your career goals. The development of your career takes time, application, and seasoning, not to mention a multitude of attributes. This book's intent is not to help you shortcut the process but perhaps to *accelerate* it through awareness and application. This starts with *you*.

Take, again, the person who "wants" to be a writer or a journalist but doesn't consistently write or tell stories through writing. Practically, this person will not likely develop writing skills over time to be in position to gain employment as a writer.

"A former mentor of mine [once] told me it was important I master one skill out of the tens it seemed I was trying to tackle at one time," says Earl Hopkins, a young journalist. "His advice rang true, as it was ultimately my abilities as a writer that separated me from my peers. Of my 10,000-hour journey, I'm probably closer to the 3,000-hour mark. And for me, understanding there's room for growth is what fosters more confidence."

If you state that you want to be a writer, but you don't write when no one is requiring writing (e.g., a classroom assignment), then you might want to reassess your pursuit of writing. If you're aspiring to be a writer and you are actually *writing*, then you're already a writer. Now it's a matter of moving toward a position where you're being paid to write (which this book can help with). If you state an aspiration to work in the film industry, but you don't have a strong "like" (if not *love*) for watching films, then an aspiration for a career in films might not coincide with your true interests. Working at a major studio may *sound* cool, but there are at least ten others with the same aspirations that *do love* film and the film industry. If you want to be a TV reporter, but don't watch/read news stories and work to develop storytelling skills, know there are 100 others who are actively working on these things. If you want to be an animator, but aren't constantly drawing or animating . . . you get the idea. The ones that succeed are doing these things when no one is watching; they read about what's going on in the industry of interest without being prompted. They retain information in an effective, efficient way because they are intrinsically engaged. I'm certain there are things like this for you.

ATTRIBUTE TIP FOR CAREER SUCCESS

ALWAYS Take the Interview

Over the years, several people have come to me seeking advice on an interview opportunity and whether they should do the interview. This is often for a position that perhaps doesn't appear to be a good fit, or the individual has recently started a new job and feels that it's not the right time to move into a new position. My answer is always "take the interview!"

Here's why. If a company or individual desires to take their own time to meet with you, then you should make every effort to do so: (1) you may like the position and the people more than you think; (2) you are making a new contact (or strengthening a current one) that could lead to an opportunity later on; and (3) you will gain experience and seasoning with interviewing, which might benefit you at some future point. It's just smart to help build your relationship network.

What if you're called for an interview when you've just accepted a position as part of your job search? That's a bit more tricky, because you don't want to *waste* someone's time or lead someone to believe that you might take the position when you clearly won't. But I would say that if you conceivably "might" take the position, then you should always take the interview.

But just as media professions tend to be nonlinear and multidimensional, so, too, may be the concept of developing your "talents" as considered through the 10,000-hour rule, which is most often considered within the nexus of a specific skill (such as a musical instrument, painting, or writing). What if you were to dedicate 10,000 hours toward the concepts found in the 12 Attributes—or at least several key ones—focusing your time and attention on whatever it is you're passionate about, reaching your goals and ambitions, dedicating time to connect with people, reading/observing the things you're most interested in, mindfully solving problems (finding solutions) within projects or activities, continuing to push forward after being rejected, putting in extra time at work to prove your trustworthiness, being open and flexible to changes (sudden or incremental), and constantly feeding your brain with stories and trends about the industry? If pure talent or a developed skill will only partially explain your successes, mastering YOU and these key attributes will be critical to your career.

Let's consider, for example, the Connective attribute, which represents the central nervous system of the model because of the importance of building meaningful relationships within media professions. Some individuals can be in a room of fifty and easily move about from person to person, able to introduce themselves and effortlessly strike up a conversation. Others find the prospect of doing this just short of terrifying. (Do you see yourself in one of those scenarios?) For the first person, this is a strength in industries that rely on networking and building connections (assuming the person is *effective* at these interactions). For the latter, this might be a "weakness" that can at least be improved upon through practice and effective strategy.

One strategy might be to meet one or two people in the course of the activity or perhaps to attend with one other person (so you don't feel as isolated while strengthening the connection with the person you're attending with). One or two great conversations might be more productive than fifty shallow ones. The key is to understand: (1) why connecting and building relationships are important; (2) what your relative strengths are in terms of being "connective"; and (3) how you might improve (or best take advantage of) the ways you connect with people.

This all requires honest self-reflection. What sounds good or "cool" to do and what you *want*—even *need*—to do to fulfill your personal goals and aspirations are often two different things. These assessments are *your* assessments, but they need to be *accurate* ones.

You and Your DMs

One way to begin to uncover your internal values and, perhaps, your deeper interests is through what I call your "defining moments." We all have experienced key moments in our lives that serve to shape—and often shift—our value systems. These can be positive, affirming moments and/or negative, even traumatic, events. Your DMs can have both positive and negative outcomes. The core of discovering a DM is that it affects you on some emotional level, which in effect hits you in a deeper, more profound way that causes change in what you do (or don't) want to do and what you will readily move toward or away from.

One DM for me is the very first vivid memory I have in life. When I was four, my grandmother lived in LA. My family drove from Hickory Ridge, Arkansas (not exactly Big City, in case you didn't know), to LA during the Christmas break. What I remember about that trip was (1) how *excited* I was about taking this trip; (2) the trip itself, making a "tent" in the floorboard of the car (pre–strict seat-belt laws); and (3) going to Universal Studios and being at Disneyland, riding the tea cups with my mom (a *big* deal) and getting my picture taken with a "security guard."

I believe my love of travel was born with this opportunity—or, perhaps, this inclination toward travel already existed within me and this was its first conscious expression. Who knows for sure? But I continue to be like a four-year-old when I travel (child-like, not child-ish). It's also not lost on me that a little boy living in an Arkansas town of 300 people eventually worked in LA in a travel-based education program (my dad was an educator, by the way). Although I've loved to travel since I was four—to my memory—it took forty-five years to integrate travel into an educational experience (for myself and others seeking a career in media). This is an expression of *who I am* and not merely what I love to do. Your professional and vocational choices, ideally, should over time evolve into expressions of your deepest values and ambitions, whatever they may be. It often takes time to get to whatever your destination is (however known or unknown it appears—but hopefully *not forty-five years*!), but it's an exciting journey worthy of pursuit.

What are *your* DMs and what do they say about you, what you move toward or away from, your aspirations, and what truly excites you? Importantly, what have been your *responses* to the DMs? You have a response-*ability* to reflect upon them honestly *and* to make the "best" of them, whatever they may be, because an effective response will make *you* better. The exercises found at the end of this attribute can help you uncover these insights. (As with all exercises and "Tips for Career Success," please *do* them!)

The Optimal You

The strongest YOU is pursuing things you believe you *have to* do along with the desire to achieve those goals. More on passion (have to) and ambition (want to) in the next two chapters. This must be self-determined—not in consideration of what your parents want, your friends are doing or think is best, and the successes or professions of others. The specific pursuits often change as you are exposed to, and/or inspired by, newly revealed interests or opportunities. Regardless, these pursuits function best when they are tied to your deepest values at any point in time.

I am far from a psychologist (but I will sometimes play one for the purposes of this book), but *accurately aware* individuals who discover their passions, pursue them with a drive to succeed, are effective at building meaningful relationships, are imaginative in approach, don't give up, maintain high relevance and reputation, and act with strong self-beliefs can achieve almost anything. This is not only an extraordinary media professional but also an extraordinary *person* who, over time, will do extraordinary things in life and career.

What are you passionate about? What *truly* makes you come alive?

YOU Exercises

1. Describe what led you to pursue a career related to media? Be *specific* in describing the people, events, content (e.g., a film, an article), personality traits, and/or moments that impacted your current aspirations (which you should also describe).

2. Your Personal Logline

   A "logline" is a term in the media industry to describe and encapsulate a story in one sentence. Provide the best description of yourself in one *carefully worded* sentence.

3a. Ranking the Attributes for *YOU* (currently)

   Among the eleven attributes provided in the model (excluding "YOU"), rank in order from 1 to 11 (with "1" being currently strongest/best and "11" being currently weakest/worst) what you believe are *your* personal attributes (*as they currently apply to your desired career*).

   _____Adaptability—*Able to adjust oneself readily to different conditions*
   _____Ambition—*Earnest desire for some type of achievement or distinction*
   _____Confidence—*Firm belief in your abilities and capacities*
   _____Connective—*Able to develop relationships and attract people, opportunities, and resources*

_____Curiosity—*Desire to continually learn or know about anything*
_____Integrity—*Adhere to moral and ethical principles*
_____Passion—*Strong affection or enthusiasm*
_____Persistent—*Refuse to give up or let go*
_____Reliability—*Dependable in completing tasks, accuracy, honesty, and so on*
_____Resilience—*Able to recover readily from hardship and adversity*
_____Resourceful—*Act effectively or imaginatively, especially in difficult situations*

3b. Ranking Your Unique Attributes

Excluding the eleven attributes above, brainstorm a list of additional qualities or attributes that apply to you. After creating your list, rank in order the Top 5 attributes (from relative "strength" to relative "weakness").

3c. Interpreting Your Attributes

Reflect on the lists created above. What do they say about you, and your own strengths and relative "weaknesses"? What types of things will you gravitate toward or away from? What do you need to improve upon?

4. Ranking Your Values

Brainstorm a list of personal values that are *important to you* (at least ten). Then rank your values starting from "most important to you" on down. What do your "hierarchy of values" tell you about your priorities?

5. The Impact of Your DMs

DMs are key events in our lives that shape our values and/or beliefs in some way. Select a DM in your life and assess its impact (1) positively and negatively, (2) then (when it happened) and now. Use the table below to express these impacts. (Note: You will likely have multiple DMs, so use the table for each one.)

Was the DM something you chose (decided by you) and/or chosen (happened due to things outside your control)? Then determine the DM's positive and negative impacts at the time of the DM and now. Think carefully and be honest in your responses.

Defining Moment: _____

Chose_____   Chosen_____

Results	Then	Now
Positive	1	1
	2	2
	3	3
	4	4
	5	5

Results	Then	Now
Negative	1	1
	2	2
	3	3
	4	4
	5	5

Passion

An irrational, yet irresistible, desire to do something

Synonyms: Love, Affection, Interest, Dedication, Devotion, Excitement

Antonyms: Apathy, Dullness, Indifference, Lethargy

Don't ask yourself what the world needs. Ask yourself what makes you come alive and go do that, because what the world needs is more people who have come alive.

—from *Wild at Heart*

Reena Dutt woke up from a dream and knew she had to do something.

The 2018 school shootings in Parkland, Florida, rocked her. She felt frustrated that nothing had changed since Columbine nearly twenty years before when she was a student at the University of Arizona.

Dutt's dream was "Too Many Bodies," a way to use her passions for film-making, music, and dance to express the "power of art as a seed for discussion." Dutt had produced John Legend's video for "Penthouse Floor," which addressed the country's political divide, and had directed or produced several films, music videos, and commercials. But nothing had moved her like this.

"I literally woke up that day and started making phone calls," she said.

Dutt had developed scores of professional relationships through her time working in New York and LA. A close friend and editor, Puppett, immediately came on board, as did Nancy Dobbs Owen, a prolific director/choreographer, who began to create choreography built around Dutt's story. Owen, also deeply affected by the shootings, began working on a dance with former students who had been touched by Alex's Mackey's "Place Called Us."

A close friend introduced Dutt to the line producer for the TV show *Teen Wolf*, who in turn called her executive producer (EP). "Yeah, give them the soundstage for a day," the EP said. "That's a great cause."

Cameras were donated, as were props for the school-based set. "Even my caterer who I've worked with on several projects and two features," Dutt recalls. "I said, 'Can I pay at cost to feed the crew and dancers?' She was like, 'no, this is a good cause. I will donate all your meals.'

"Everyone I called was like 'how can I help?'" Dutt says. "It wasn't pulling teeth. It wasn't trying too hard."

Dutt soon put together a deck of reference images to gather her ideas of what she had seen in her dream. She showed it to people and began to put bios together of those friends who had agreed to join the project. Her dream (literally and figuratively) to foster "the conversation about gun violence" through her art was soon to became a reality.

An early screening of "Too Many Bodies" at Art of Elysium, an LA organization that supports individuals with a variety of emotional life challenges, left the room in silence, except for sounds of crying. The film was soon screened all around the United States, particularly at festivals in states where gun reform is a challenging topic of discussion. The team also built an advocacy and support website to further use her work as a platform for emotional support and social change.

"Everybody has different ideas and different interests," Dutt says. "But with any thought there are multiple people with similar thoughts, and it's just a matter of putting it out there. A part of me feels like that's what materializes these passion projects at the end of the day. You'll find your people. And people are good at heart. They too want a sense of belonging and understanding from the stories they tell."

"That's why I love filmmaking," Dutt says. "It's a magical way to communicate and relate to each other."[1]

Think of someone you know who has a strong passion for something. What do you notice about the person when they engage in some way with the passion (e.g., talking about it, working at it)? Does the person speak and act with more enthusiasm and energy? Do they smile more? Sit or stand up straighter? Is it difficult to get them to talk about the object of interest? (It's often hard to get them to shut up, right?) Do they invest a lot of time in service of this passion? Does everything go perfectly or smoothly for a person engaging in the passion? And, what do you notice about *you* in the presence of someone expressing or enacting their passion? Do you look forward to seeing them (maybe not if you can't get them to shut up!)? Even if you don't share the same passion, are you nevertheless drawn to the person enacting or expressing the passion?

Now picture someone who is *dis*passionate about something. This person might be real or imagined. What is that person's posture? Is there a lilt to their voice? Is the person smiling? Do they demonstrate enthusiasm about the object or topic? Do you look forward to your encounters with them? Does good fortune seem to fall their way? Does the person *feel* lucky or expect good results?

If you think about it, passion is a curious word to be associated with our work lives. Passion is a word of *love*, a deeply internalized emotional expression that represents the nature of creation itself (both biologically and creatively). I personally know physicians, accountants, engineers, teachers, contractors, landscapers, and of course, media professionals who display a passion for their work. They are usually really good at what they do and exhibit a certain joy for the process and outcomes associated with their passion. They are not always happy; they have faced challenges and struggles—even heartbreak—but they feel "lucky" to be doing what they're doing. What's behind all of this?

Why Passion Matters for Your Career

When I ask successful media professionals to express the qualities or attributes most important in a career, the first answer more times than not is "passion" ("you've gotta have a passion for it"). Although passion would be a positive for almost any endeavor, careers in media almost seem to *demand* passion as a requisite quality for success. Yet there is very little actual discourse about what the word means, why passion is important, how/where it develops, and how passion serves career development and success.

Media professions are far too competitive and unpredictable to "suffer" those who lack a passion or desire for what they do. The hours are often long and unstructured, employment is often uncertain, and there's a constant social component at play in collaborative settings. The expected early career mismatches between what you aspire to do and what you're actually doing often present a challenge. In order to *thrive* (not just survive) within this thicket of obstacles, an internalized love becomes important. Those with a passion for a profession or a pursuit demonstrate a love for what they do and often can't see themselves doing anything else, just as some people can't see themselves with any*one* else. But what is passion in pursuit of? Is it a specific outcome? Is it an "idea" or "idealized" pursuit or reality?

I absolutely love the definition of passion provided at the beginning of this attribute ("an irrational yet irresistible desire to do something")! Media and entertainment professions aren't rational to a lot of other people. It kind of *is* irrational to pursue a career with such unpredictability that so heavily relies on the creation of "products" from the minds and efforts of unseen people. Your family and friends often don't understand why you're willing to pursue challenges wrought with so much uncertainty when more predictable avenues exist.

Of equal relevance in that definition is the word "irresistible"—you're drawn toward an object or pursuit in a way you can't resist. If you're truly, genuinely, drawn toward interests that you can't resist, you're more likely to *persist* in your efforts to get wherever the pursuits might lead you. This irresistible-ness will automatically add energy to your pursuits. As the "irrational yet irresistible" *ensues*, you'll care less and less about what others think; you'll use the doubters as fuel toward positive outcomes (in a competitive, not vengeful, way). Your time and positive energy will be in the service of the pursuits you really love.

ATTRIBUTE TIP FOR CAREER SUCCESS

Be an Energy Giver

When my beloved Kansas City Royals went to back-to-back World Series in 2014–2015, General Manager (GM) Dayton Moore shared how a specific evaluation criterion factored into the organization's success. Scouts, on their check sheets for potential players or draftees, marked whether they observed the individual to be an "energy giver" or an "energy sucker." Those deemed energy suckers were automatically discarded from consideration, regardless of talent level, because of an expectation that the attitude would serve to bring down the team. Energy *givers* obviously needed requisite skills and talent but were additionally valued for how they might contribute to the team and organization in a way that extends beyond the individual contribution.[2]

Because media professions are highly collaborative and social, people tend to hire (or bring onto projects) others they like to be around. Those who are energy givers do just that: they add energy to the collaboration or group and gain value because of that. They keep the mood positive when the hours get long or when there's a delay. They make time better for others. This doesn't imply that "adding energy" is more important than being highly competent, but energy givers will be hired over energy suckers almost every time if the level of competence is close.

You have undoubtedly been around both energy givers and energy suckers. Who would you rather spend a twelve-hour day with? The answer is obvious. Media and creative professionals value people who bring a positive attitude and energy. Be aware of this when you're in a group or organization. If you're an energy giver, people will want you to be in their company (literally and figuratively), and you'll automatically connect with others through the positive energy you bring.

What are some things *you* are REALLY passionate about? What makes you "come alive," as the quote from *Wild at Heart* (my own personal mantra) urges us to do? Jot down a few of your passions. What are things that the very mention of gets you excited and engage your mind and *heart* in a way that allows you to process information—and commit to memory—at an uncommonly high level? How do you know this? Do you spend your own time in pursuit of things related to your passion? When you talk about your passions with others, do you speak faster? Does your inflection change? Are you more likely to seek out people with similar interests? Your answers need not be media-related and need not make sense to anyone else. This should be *your* answer, tied to *your* interests and, possibly (but not necessarily), *your* aspirations. If you're truly passionate about those objects or pursuits, the answer to each question is a resounding "Yes!"

These reflections about what makes you come alive should tell you a lot about yourself and what you're willing to invest your time and energy toward. If, for example, you are passionate about sports, perhaps your career pursuits should be directed toward some area of sports. In the media industries, this might be sports production, sports management, or public relations. (Or perhaps your love of sports is such that you prefer to keep it separated from your professional life.) What if your passion is fashion (cool rhyme!)? Where might you direct your interests toward building a successful career? What if you have a passion—or deep abiding interest—for movies? What if you have a passion for telling stories? What if you love making people laugh? Getting a reaction? What if you love building successful teams and collaborating with people? Where and how might you direct these interests into an actual career? When you're highly engaged in an interest when no one else is looking or when no one is expecting something in exchange, you're pursuing your passion.

Regardless, understanding what you're passionate about offers an important key to your media-related career. As a practical matter, passion matters because: (1) you'll work harder—and probably *smarter*—when your pursuits are connected to your interests and deeper values; (2) you'll retain information more effectively and efficiently with a thirst to know more; (3) you'll draw people to you because they'll be attracted to your passion (even if they don't have the same specific passion), and you'll be more likely to attract their time and attention through your natural enthusiasm; (4) you'll be more likely to persist through struggles and disappointments in pursuits you love; and, critically, (5) a lot of the "work" (synonyms of which are "labor," "toil," and "drudgery"—yuck!) won't feel so much like work to you when you're doing something intrinsically tied to your deeper interests.

It's nearly impossible for me to imagine a "dispassionate" media professional being able to advance and achieve at a high level. (There are people who create a long media career without having a passion, but this book has *extraordinary* in the title, so that's the basis we're working upon.) And why would you even want to? It's all too difficult an undertaking if you don't really have a strong interest in it.

This is not to imply that every day will be rosy and your early career and internship experiences, at times, will most certainly feel uninspiring, if not like downright drudgery. You won't likely "love" every part of your job. But this is the vital reason why having a passion for a pursuit, whether specific or more general, is critical. Your passions will help enable you to see your way clear of the obstacles through a positive attitude and an open spirit. As one of my great former students, Samantha Bloomfield, once told me, "I'm not necessarily passionate about picking up lunches every single day, but I *am* passionate about working in TV, and I know that being a good PA is my avenue to keep doing that, so I'm never going to complain about it."

Just as important, *others* will notice this in you, and your ability to maintain positive energy will demonstrate your viability for a successful career in the longer term. If you're in pursuit of your deeper passions *with* passion, I believe that resulting successes will ensue over time. The process of getting there will yield its own intrinsic rewards and benefits. Some you can anticipate; some will be completely unexpected. Be excited about that notion. Trust that you'll look back with pride that you pursued the things you're passionate about.

Why Media Professionals Are Passionate about What They Do

On a whim one Saturday morning in LA, I asked my friends on Facebook to volunteer answers to the following question: Why do you have a passion for what you do? I received dozens of responses, and they are revealing. Here is a sample from media professionals:

Casting Director: I get to fall in love with people every day! Finding the right person for a role or project brings me so much joy! It's like treasure hunting!

Reality Producer: It's exciting to hear the audience reaction to my work (whether it's in person or via Twitter comments!). I love creating something that causes an emotional response, laughter, tears, excitement, or inspiration.

Sportswriter: I get to meet all sorts of people and I get to tell their stories.

Producer: I am passionate because what I do allows me to take a thought or an idea and make it real. I love bringing people together of different skill sets and backgrounds to focus on a goal together, and enjoying the ride as we go.

Journalist: Every day is different. You get to meet the most amazing people, see the most amazing places, and tell heartfelt stories. I get to work with a diverse group of smart people who all share the same passion. We get a front row seat to history and experience it together.

Corporate Video Producer/Director: Once I was assigned to produce and direct a short video explaining a new state policy regarding the foster care system. Part of the project involved a scripted scenario showing two young adults just out of foster care, but the two characters were portrayed by actual young people who had just gotten out of foster care. They'd scripted the video as well. Anyway, on the day of filming, I was cranky and tired but the shoot went remarkably well and afterward one of the "actors" came up to me and said, "Thank you, you really made us feel important." Stuff like that doesn't happen a lot, but if it happens enough, it's not hard to stay passionate about the job.

Regional Radio Station Rep: I love being part of a world most don't think about and helping make a difference with the stations we work with. It can come down to the well-above-average customer service or even having a genuine "un-corporate" type conversation in which the relationship I build makes my job that much more enjoyable!

Mixing Engineer: Mixing has become almost an extension of my brain. I feel most comfortable when exercising that extension of my brain. Hearing a transformation of an edit to a finished product is extremely rewarding.

Production Manager: It's hard not to be passionate about being in a media industry. Nothing in our society is considered successful if others don't know about it. Content and stories are the ways we judge ourselves against our peers, our colleagues, and our competition. The media industry touches every other industry in the world. Being a part of it allows me to connect with so many different people from all walks of life, experience different kinds of products, learn about cutting-edge research, listen to opposing opinions. It allows me the chance to travel, and a chance to tell others of my experiences. . . . There are few other careers that allow for as much people to people interaction as media do. At the end of the day it brings me quite a bit of satisfaction knowing my input helped shape someone else's thoughts, opinions, and beliefs; sometimes in a small way, and sometimes in a largely impactful way. I think it requires great integrity and thought when approaching any decision in this industry.

And you won't be surprised that passion can also be found in non-media professions . . .

Financial Advisor: I LOVE my career. I'm independent so I feel like I can truly give the absolute best advice to my clients based upon their goals, wants, and needs without being tied to a specific company. I am super passionate about my career because I am constantly helping people. I love being of service.

Landscape Designer: Designing has always been my passion as well as working outside in the landscape. It makes me feel so close to God, with all the colors and wonder there is to find in the wonderful outdoors. Doing what I do for a living fills my soul as well as my passion. How lucky you are if you can get up each day to get paid for doing something you truly LOVE.

Professor: My passion is the "aha!" moment. Eliciting in myself and students that split second when a "light bulb" turns on—that new awareness—large or small—that fresh understanding takes place that once it happens cannot easily be extinguished.

Human Resources Professional: I am passionate about changing the future of the workplace to better reflect how human needs are evolving. Everyone should be able to feel valued in an org, company, or a startup and have that excitement from making an impact, but there are so many factors that stall the ship. My passion and purpose is to help people/companies work through those and move ahead strategically and empathetically with humor as well.

Scholar/Writer: I am passionate about writing the "everyday" . . . I find it magical when I can use words to piece together people's (and my own) experiences. What is more magical is when someone reads my writing and says, "This is what I was thinking, but did not know how to say it."

Do you see a consistent pattern in the aforementioned diverse occupations? People want to feel connected, to be of value to others, to contribute, to make an impact, to get a reaction, to feel valued, and to do something larger than themselves. Notice also how true passion seems to transcend money and title. All of the people above *feel* successful—*are* successful—because the work is connected intrinsically to their interests and deeper values. They don't think of it as "work." But rest assured, they all work very hard and make a very good living in the process of connecting who they are with their passions.

Regardless of vocation, there are immense direct and indirect benefits to enacting your passions as a habit for your life. As Jeff Bridges stated during his acceptance of an honorary award at the 2019 Golden Globes, your passion and positive energy can "tag" someone and make a real difference. The same is true for you and how you impact others when they see passion in you. They are attracted to you, more likely to want to be around you, and will value your involvement.

Simply put, your passions, whatever they are, add value to the world.

Developing Passion in Your Career: Don't "Find" It—*Grow* It!

You might or might not have a strong idea of exactly what you want to do in your career. If you don't, that's okay because passion clearly transcends any single vocation. As you'll see next, a broader perspective about your interests and aspirations might carry important advantages for your career development.

Our passions develop from a mix of genetic and environmental factors. We're inclined to love what we're good at, and our innate skills are a product, at least to some degree, of our genes. Dean Simonton of the University of California at Davis found that 22 to 36 percent of creative successes are potentially due to our genetic skills (i.e., what we're born with).[3] Although a significant percentage, this also implies that far more than the majority of what we're inclined to do is explained by factors other than genetics, such as environment, practice, exposure, and motivation.

The professions or vocations we choose are thought to be the combination of an individual's interests, abilities, and personality characteristics. John Holland theorizes that vocational choice isn't independent of personality, but actually exists as an expression of one's personality, interests, and goals.[4] When a mismatch occurs across any one of these variables, one is left dissatisfied with the result.

Could this help explain why about two-thirds of the U.S. working population dislikes their jobs? This also helps explain why pure cognitive ability (whether measured by GPA or IQ) or having a developed skill is not usually, in and of itself, sufficient for success in media and creative professions. The pathways are too messy, competition is too stiff, and relationships are too important to rely strictly on a skill or pure intelligence to reach a goal. However, when someone's abilities are tied to their interests and personality within their vocation/profession, then their abilities are synced up with these pursuits and the odds of successful outcomes increase. An obvious challenge, however, is that your interests and abilities won't be always—even often—be in sync with what you're doing, especially early in your career. This is all the more reason to have passion in your suitcase of attributes. A clear notion of what you're really passionate about will help you see past the obstacles you'll encounter and will help keep you motivated.

Self-Determination Theory, a popular and verified hypothesis, states that passion is built on three factors:

(1) *autonomy*—the ability to control involvement in the activity (control over how you fill your time);
(2) *competence*—the ability to do something well (mastering unambiguously useful things and to attain valued outcomes within the pursuits); and
(3) *relatedness*—ability to collaborate and connect with your coworkers and community (feeling of connection to others).

An activity or career that meets these three criteria is a good sign that this could be a passion worth investing in. The article "Beyond Passion: The Science of Loving What You Do" states it well: "Once you have something valuable to offer, use it to gain as much autonomy, competence, and relatedness as you can possibly cram into your life."[5]

Unfortunately, though with good intention, college students and aspiring professionals are challenged to "find" their passions. We want people we love and care about to be happy, to "love what you do for a living," and not to bow to pressures for status or money. But is "finding" your passion the most beneficial way to *develop* your passion?

According to researchers, expecting to "find your passion" might actually undermine this well-intentioned imperative. A "fixed mindset," such as a belief that a passion for a specific profession is something to be "found," is significantly more likely to hold people back. Why? Those with a fixed mindset are more likely to (1) expect things to be easy (e.g., expect to be endlessly motivated by their passion for a given field), (2) lose interest more easily (e.g., give up when the going gets tough), and (3) be less open to new fields (e.g., find little reason to explore new areas).[6]

Thus, finding your passion is not a bad thing; *expecting* to find your passion protects you from reality. In other words, being locked into a passion often misleads people to think that the passion itself offers endless motivation and less difficulty with the added whammy of discounting potential new interests. In a sense, urging people to find their passion may lead them to put all their eggs in one basket but then to drop that basket when it becomes difficult to carry.[7] We are likely to believe that our deeply internalized interests should provide constant motivation and inspiration, making engagement and involvement with the interest relatively easy with minimal difficulty or frustration.

What might be a better mindset? The answer is one oriented toward "growth." With a growth mindset you'll be more likely to keep working at it, to keep practicing—to *grow* your passion—*and* to be more open to exploring fields outside your own. Whereas a fixed mindset might lead you to conclude that you aren't passionate about the pursuit after all, a growth orientation means that you find intrinsic interest in development of your skills. Plus, you'll believe that having a strong interest in one area does not preclude you from developing interests elsewhere, some of which might enrich or extend your passions or lead to new, unanticipated ones.[8]

ATTRIBUTE TIP FOR CAREER SUCCESS

Do Projects on the Side

Early career jobs aren't likely to be exactly what you aspire to do, so it's important to take initiative to gain experience doing the things you see yourself eventually doing. Smart young and aspiring professionals do projects outside of work or class. This might be to shoot a short film or music video, volunteer to help lead the marketing effort for a local charity or organization, produce and perform music wherever you're allowed, or many other things. These side projects additionally build your skills to think resourcefully, to be proactive, and to connect with people with similar interests. You won't likely have much or any money; you'll have to persuade restaurants or locations or bars to give you access; you'll have to find a way to access equipment or resources. All of these, in the service of your longer-term interests, "grow" your passions while building your hard skills. You'll become more "seasoned" in the process and be more ready for opportunities in the future.

Think about how this factors into early career activities in media professions that might be mundane, less than inspiring, and beneath your education level. Let's say you are "fixed" on becoming a writer. It is highly unlikely that you will earn a living as a writer, perhaps for several years. A fixed mindset (or "passion") may lead you to give up more quickly out of frustration because you're not seeing the fruits of your efforts and perhaps will close off opportunities in related areas or toward things that might help feed or enhance your writing skills. If, however, you see yourself becoming a paid, professional writer as part of personal development in service of growth, you'll be more willing to assume an open, big-picture view about the process, and you'll be more likely to grow your passion over time. The same is true for an aspiring news reporter, who might aspire to work at a national network but invariably starts in local market #183. Or an aspiring director of photography (DP), who wants to work on feature films but must invariably apprentice as a second assistant camera (AC) for a couple of years (at least) before becoming a first AC for a few years before maybe becoming a DP.

The bigger point is that to become really good and accomplished at something, things *will* get tough at times. There will be challenges and struggles. There *should* be challenges and struggles. How do you really know you're passionate about something if you haven't encountered some difficulty along the way? Moreover, you might not honestly yet be "ready" to successfully handle what the fixed outcome might be. Are you really ready to be in a writer's room with twenty-year veterans? Are you seasoned enough as a journalist or reporter to handle the pressure of the national stage? Do you really know enough about lenses and lighting to be in charge of a feature film? A growth mindset connected to your interests will help get you there *better* because you'll focus on your own development so that you are ready when opportunity strikes, you'll anticipate that pursuing a passion will sometimes be difficult, and you'll also be more open to other avenues that may emerge as equally or more inspiring.

This last point is critical. It's important to keep in mind that many successful people, especially in media-related professions, wind up doing something very different from what they set out to do. The real passion might lie in the desire to grow and develop, rather than to accomplish a predetermined skill or outcome. Openness to new interests can often create new opportunities for learning. Be careful not to misplace your passion onto a fixed outcome, but rather focus your interests into the kind of life you seek to build for yourself.

A limited range of interests is not in itself a liability and may, in some circumstances, reduce distraction as you develop a skill. But one of the biggest red flags I hear from college students is "I just want to direct (films)" or "I just want to be an anchor" or "I just want to make music." The red flag is the inference that all other subjects are irrelevant. This can serve to short-circuit development of skills and attributes that might be critical to help feed and grow your passion, especially when you must integrate ideas from diverse sources to create content.

The focus on process, rather than immediate results, can be difficult to grasp in our culture because we are often focused on the outcome at the expense of what's to be gained along the way. We want to see the manifestation of our time and efforts. But it's in the *process* where the real long-term, sustaining *growth* and development manifests itself.

So, the question again is: What are you *really* passionate about? What makes you come alive? Is it an outcome? A process? An idea? An involvement? To influence? Why is it meaningful to you? Why does it make your heart skip a beat? Why is it worth the occasional heartache (or heartburn)? What do you really seek to gain from it?

Remember, your passion is *your* passion. Whatever it is and however it developed, it is yours. Follow it—don't discount it—grow it, nurture it, and seek to connect it in some meaningful way to your goals and aspirations, whatever they might be. When you have a passion for something, you'll invest more time and positive energy toward that pursuit, and, more times than not, the investment of time and energy will have a positive outcome for you and others, even if that might take you in new, unexpected directions.

Perhaps even more important, show the world that you're "capable" of being passionate about anything. Choose what you do for your own reasons then strive to be great at it and have a positive attitude along the way. The specifics will emerge on their own terms and in their own ways. I'm struck by how successful people talk with excitement and energy about what they do and have a great enthusiasm to *share* what they do and know.

Although some people undoubtedly possess innate talent, the greater "gift" is most likely the passion and drive that manifests those talents, whatever they are. Talent without a passion or desire to develop it won't get you far; passion with modest talents will lead you to *something* of value, often of high value, even if that "something" is not fully known at this moment.

PASSION Exercises

1. Make a list of two to four things in your life that you consider to be your passions. For each describe:

   a. How/why the passion developed/when did it start?
   b. What specific behaviors tell you that this is a passion of yours (e.g., time working, thinking, or talking)?
   c. How might each passion—even if indirectly—relate to your career interests?

2. Start a conversation with someone you know about something they *really* love (ideally in the media/creative industries, but doesn't need to be). Include as part of your questioning:

   a. When/how did your passion start?
   b. How do you know this is your passion?
   c. How much time do you spend thinking and/or working on your passion?
   d. How does your passion enhance your life?

    e. What types of frustrations or challenges do you encounter, if any, with your passion?

What do you notice about the person when they are talking about the passion? Take note and be specific.

3. Identify a person you know that you consider to be an "energy giver," and another person you consider to be an "energy sucker." Describe the specific behaviors of each that lead you to each respective conclusion?

Ambition

An earnest desire for some type of achievement or distinction, and the willingness to strive for its attainment

Synonyms: Aspiration, Yearning, Goal, Strive, Drive, Vision

Antonyms: Apathy, Idleness, Contentment, Complacency, Entitlement

Ambition is not what you would do, but what you do, for ambition without action is fantasy.

—Bryant McGill

During my first teaching job, I taught a sophomore-level course called "The Business of Media." As I always do on the first day of class, I went around the room and asked students to introduce themselves and state what they would *really* like to do in the profession. Starting along the back row and working toward me, students expressed a variety of interests, such as being a writer, cinematographer, music producer, film director, and so on. A few said they "don't know."

Now on the fourth row from the front, I pointed at a tall dark-haired student, who said, "I'm John Anderson and my dream job is to write for Conan O'Brien." The specificity of the answer struck me, so I followed up by asking "why."

"Because his comedy is brilliant and I want to write comedy," John replied.

Making my way down to the next row, I motioned toward another student. "I'm Andrew Hamer." Andrew turned slightly and directed his thumb to the person directly behind him. "And I want to do what he said."

The class laughed. I asked Andrew if he had anything to add to what John had said.

"No." This brought more laughter. "I never seriously thought about what I actually wanted to do with my degree until now."

As soon as the class ended, Andrew followed John out of the classroom, and they struck up a conversation. Soon after they joined with a third student, Rich Baker, to form Senseless Acts of Comedy, an improvisation troupe that soon began to perform free shows each Thursday night.

Andrew, John, and Rich found four other students with similar interests. They distributed flyers and told friends and family to come. At first, the shows lacked polish and contained some painful moments. However, as time went on and the group kept at it, they became better. Word soon got around and attendance grew. What started in an eighty-seat classroom soon moved to a 150-seat auditorium. Soon that auditorium was overflowing on most Thursday nights and had become a weekly campus event. Finally, during the last semester of school, the shows moved to a nearby theater that continued to overflow despite the increased capacity. As the "guys" continued to develop their talents, they began to land professional improv and stand-up comedy jobs in Dallas.

After a show one night late in his senior year, Andrew told me, "I can't wait to go to Second City. I feel like I'm starting all over again. I'm going to learn how to do this a new way, and with so many new experiences. I know I have a long way to go, but I'm so excited about jumping into this."

For anyone, especially a twenty-two-year-old, this was an exceptional perspective. Andrew and his friends had turned Senseless Acts of Comedy into a weekly event and parlayed their talents into professional experiences. And yet Andrew knew there was more growth to come. He was excited about the process ahead. Andrew and his friends had not only found their passion but also developed a vision of what they wanted to do.

Dream Big, Work Hard . . . and You'll Get Wherever "There" Is

Consider the following questions:

> What would be your dream job if there were *no* obstacles in your way?
> Do you tell others what your dreams are?
> What would give your life *meaning and purpose* on the way to achieving it?

If you're starting your career (or about to), your loftier aspirations might seem a bit unattainable at this point. Or, in reading this book so far, you might be a bit overwhelmed, even intimidated, to consider how you will get from Point A to Point Z, wherever and whatever that is, because the roadmap seems so uncertain and unclear and unpredictable.

Don't fear. Be excited.

What we become in the process of our achievements is more important than what we "get" in the outcome, just as happiness and success are best when they ensue from what you're compelled to do rather than in direct pursuit of money and title.

So dream big. It's important. It's what the world needs.

Media-related professions are inherently made for dreamers and big dreams. You're involved in creating and telling stories, sometimes even creating "worlds," and you seek to connect your work with a larger public that wants to be moved or informed by you in some compelling way. How could you not have some big ideas about your life within these professions!?!

And if you worry about what others think about your dreams, don't worry so much. In fact, *let them know*. Let *them* exist in the practical world if that's not your cup of tea.

Your ambitions are best manifest through your imagination, a uniquely human endowment that allows you to visualize a compelling future and then craft a plan to attain it. Lofty aspirations help fuel your growth and propel you beyond where—and who—you presently are.

Media professions are heavily populated with strivers: people anxious to do more, to move up the ranks or to a bigger market, to gain access to the resources that allow their passions to be manifest into some type of tangible reality (e.g., an article, a TV series, a feature film, a newscast, a podcast). But the media professions are also populated, especially near the beginner ranks, with people who are attracted to the allure of public industries but often lack the true passion and/or the abiding ambition to make their dreams a reality.

ATTRIBUTE TIP FOR CAREER SUCCESS

Don't Try to Advance Too Fast

I once asked veteran television producer Kevin Hamburger, "What's the biggest mistake young media professionals make?"

"Trying to advance too fast," Hamburger told me. "I see young people trying to leap past people who've been working for years at their craft, and that's almost never a good thing. There's often a backlash toward those trying to move up before they're really ready."

We all want to attain our definition of success quickly and with as little resistance as possible. But you will need others on your pathway to success, and your reputation will be built on your willingness to work hard and smart with others. Seek to *accelerate* your progress through focus and application of the various attributes and your own work ethic, but be careful to not try to blow past the process that may have taken others, even perhaps the most successful people, years upon years to get to. You might not be as ready as you think you are *now*, and your willingness to build your career through experience and relationships will benefit you in the long run.

If you try to advance too fast, with little to no consideration of the people you're working with, you will leave remnants of your actions behind, which may, in turn, block your next potential opportunity. When you're *really* ready, opportunities and access will come your way.

Extraordinary media professionals succeed over the long term because they don't allow the voices of practicality to interfere with what they really want. They connect their passions, the essential *have to*, with a drive to achieve their dreams. They think big. They act toward big things. And they become big over time.

Most of all, they *work at it*. They put in the hours. They keep moving forward, even when knocked sideways; they challenge themselves; they are able to see things others don't; they learn from their mistakes (of which there are many); they act with purpose; they are *never* complacent, and they remain open to new, unexpected ways to grow and achieve. They also treat people fairly along the way if they are truly extraordinary.

You don't have to be Oprah, Spielberg, Lady Gaga, Jay-Z, or Seinfeld to be extraordinary, and you shouldn't seek to be *them*, but your ambitions should be most connected to what you want your life and career to be about, not what our culture or your peers deem as valuable or practical. At the same time, you should challenge yourself to determine what your dreams are and begin to act on them. As Walt Disney once said, "All of our dreams can come true, if we have the courage to pursue them."

Although you shouldn't feel pressured to know exactly what you want to do, it does *help to have an idea*! When aspiring professionals tell me, for example, "I don't know exactly what I want to do, but I just know I want to tell stories," I think that's a *great* answer. The subtext of the answer is that the aspirant (1) has an interest, (2) is pointed in a direction, and (3) has a growth mindset about finding what is interesting and exciting within the field.

Compare this to a different perspective: "I only want to direct films." This aspirant, with a few hyper-focused exceptions like Spielberg and Scorsese, might be in trouble. The subtext of the answer is that only classes and experiences connected to film directing are relevant, and important avenues of thought, such as understanding the business, developing important relationships, considering social impact of what they will do, and more broad non-media subjects that might aid the storytelling process, do not hold interest or are of little value. This "fixed" mindset might not be in that person's best developmental interests. If you think you're as hyper-focused as Spielberg, just make sure you really are.

Our *professional* ambitions ultimately need to be more than an idea or an interest. Working in concert with your passion for something, your ambitions give you that compelling "carrot" that dangles in front of you to pull you forward. Your ambitions should connect to internalized and external goals that matter to you and your own personal growth and development and yet be grounded in a strong willingness to take steps necessary to make it happen. This is particularly vital early in your career because of unpredictable pathways we've already detailed. Few achieve their grand ambitions early in the career, and that's probably for the better for you in The Big Picture. Your process toward self-actualization, whatever that is for you in the media professions and in life, should not happen too easily and neatly (even though that sounds appealing in the moment).

The key is to remain *motivated* to search and strive for more. In The Big Picture, the results we "get" at the end of a process can sometimes seem oddly, yet wonderfully, misaligned with what ensues. Herb Trawick of *Pensado's Place* literally could not conceive when he was a successful music producer/manager in the 1980s that he would, in his late fifties, cohost a popular YouTube show that's become a seven-figure business. But it all played a part in his Big Picture.

Your own career is a *process* of development that includes building your skills, refining those talents, and enacting the important attributes that help connect you with people and resources that lead you closer to the things you aspire toward. This happens incrementally, not instantly, for almost everyone. And that's how it should be.

Two Key Ways to Take Action Now toward Your Ambitions

Find Professional Mentors

As much as I believe in the power of "process" as part of your career development and "owning" your career, I also don't believe in reinventing the wheel. One of the best ways to foster your ambitions is to engage with successful people who are connected in some way to your own interests and aspirations. Those who have experienced the media industry, including its ups and downs, can help guide you and, perhaps, help you avoid at least a few of the unnecessary potholes on your own road to success.

In my experience and observation, many successful media professionals are willing to give time to those who show an interest in what they do. You typically have to schedule this more around *their* time, but you might be surprised by who is willing to talk with you, especially as we are now so accustomed to the relative convenience of video chats (Zoom, Teams, Google Hangout).

These professional mentors often see a younger version of themselves in you ("How successful would I be if I had someone in my position that helped me when I first started") and/or were helped in significant ways by professional role models and seek to pay it forward. They take pleasure—even pride—in helping foster your career development. Many successful people, as they see you as someone with a deep, abiding passion and a continuing interest to learn, will be flattered that you're seeking them out as a resource of knowledge, perspective, and advice.

You potentially have so much to gain as key professional mentors give you "inside insight" into the work and commitment needed to become successful. This will enhance your own confidence and help provide some clarity to what you do and *don't* want to do career-wise (both distinctions will be important). You will have opportunities to make additional contacts within the industry, possibly find jobs/internships, or become aware of industry-related organizations or resources that may benefit you.

Importantly, this relationship is often *mutually beneficial*; you're not just the "taker" in this relationship. Your key professional contacts gain the satisfaction of "giving back" through time and sharing knowledge/perspective about the career. The mentor also gets an opportunity to stop and reflect/articulate what they do, which often becomes difficult in the busy lives of successful media professionals. The *mentor* will become better at understanding their own career and purpose through the opportunity to communicate this with you.[1]

Whether you label this person a "mentor" or a "key professional resource" is less important than finding great role models to learn from and engage with on a regular basis. (*Important:* Don't formally ask the people to be your mentor. Let it be their idea. Otherwise, the busy professional might be a bit scared off by the perceived commitment of time.) But try to find one or two key ones that assume a special interest in your career and development. The big key to your success will be the development of important relationships (more on this in the next attribute) along all rungs of the success ladder, but early on, connecting with someone who is a bit "up there" can be very beneficial and powerful.

So how do you actually go about getting a professional mentor/resource? Unless you already know the person, don't expect someone to be your "mentor" right away. Instead, start by asking for information meetings with successful people where you seek to learn more about what they do. Contact them directly or, even better, let one of your current contacts make an introduction for you. If you meet the successful person at a social gathering, be sure to follow up with an email and ask if you might have an informational meeting *at their convenience*. After the first meeting or two, ask, "Could we meet periodically, at your convenience, so that I can learn more about what you do and get your advice?" Most are flattered if you approach them with a bit of deference. If the other person offers to be your mentor—actually says the word "mentor"—and you feel good about it, even better!

Again, you'll learn more about the critical importance of building relationships in the next chapter, but your ambitions are fostered through key successful contacts that can help "show you the way."

Set Formal Goals

One key way to help activate your ambitions for the media professions is through goal setting. Writing down your goals serves, for you, as a "contract" to help keep you moving forward to develop the skills, knowledge, and attributes needed to succeed in the short and long term. Think of your long-term goals as the "carrot" to pull you forward and your short-term goals as the "stick" to keep you motivated on a consistent basis.

Look at this great definition of goal setting:

Process of identifying something that you want to accomplish and establishing measurable goals and timeframes.

That's all you need to know: (1) process, (2) finding what you want, (3) establishing goals you can measure, and (4) setting a deadline for yourself.

Easy-peasy, right?

Setting goals sounds good, but shockingly few people actually do this and even fewer write them down (less than 10 percent of adults!).[2] The evidence is overwhelming that written goals lead to significant benefits (financial and satisfaction) versus those that don't have goals or simply "think" their goals.[3] There is something powerful about writing down what you seek to achieve in the short and long terms to help keep your eye—and spirit—focused on the bigger achievements and distinctions you strive for.

ATTRIBUTE TIP FOR CAREER SUCCESS

How to Handle the "Five-Year" Question

The following is a common interview question: "Where do you see yourself in five years?" This is an exceedingly difficult question to actually answer because of the variable paths one can take and five years can feel like an eternity given the number of technological, structural, and taste-related unknowns. You don't want to shoot too high or too low, so what do you say?

Bruce Dunn, a long-time GM and producer, gave the best answer I've heard when asked by an aspiring media professional how to answer this question in an interview: "I would say, 'I want to be sitting at the table where decisions are being made.'"

This answer might not apply to all professional aspirations, and you should consider it within your own values and goals, but it's a good way to think about this answer in terms of giving it if asked and in terms of your own career.

The subtext of the answer is that you are willing to work hard and smart over a period of time in which you will develop the reputation, skills, and relationships that *earn* a spot "at the table."

So why don't more people write down their goals? Some simply don't have them. For some, it feels like too much effort. Others think goal setting is self-limiting (i.e., setting a goal somehow limits possibility). Some others have tried goal setting unsuccessfully (or perhaps didn't employ them effectively). Some don't want to be accountable for themselves. Goal setting does take some practice—it's not necessarily easy to do effectively—but can be *critical* if you want to achieve your ambitions.

Aspiring or working media professionals might view goal setting as particularly difficult to undertake due to the nonlinear and uncertain nature of the professions. This is all the more reason to write down your goals, pay attention to them, adjust them when necessary, and then take consistent steps to meet your ongoing goals and larger aspirations. Your uniquely human endowment to visualize helps pull you forward to whatever that great "last job" might be. And, although your "first jobs" might continue to be crummy and beneath your education level, your last-job perspective might help you accelerate just a little more quickly to the next jobs.

SIX REASONS WHY YOU NEED TO SET GOALS[4]

1. **Goals Propel You Forward**—Having a goal written down with a set date for accomplishment gives you something to plan and work for.
2. **Goals Transform Insurmountable Mountains into Walkable Hills**—Proper goal setting can help break larger, intimidating aspirations into smaller, more achievable stepping stones. It is easier to formulate a definite plan of action to work on right away. Hitting smaller milestones provides real motivation and greater contentment.
3. **Goals Help Us Believe in Ourselves**—Setting goals is a way to fuel your ambition. Goal setting isn't just about creating a plan for your life and holding yourself accountable; it's also about giving the inspiration necessary to aim for things we never thought possible. Unless you make it a goal for yourself and work every day toward achieving it, why would you ever believe that you could accomplish it?
4. **Goals Hold You Accountable for Failure**—If you don't write down concrete goals and give yourself a timeline for achievement, how can you look back and re-evaluate your path if you fail? It's a concrete sign that whatever you're doing isn't working, and you need to make real changes if you want to get where you want to be.
5. **Goals Tell You What You Truly Want**—If you never set goals in the first place, how do you find out what you truly want? By asking ourselves what we really want and constantly

reassessing our goals, we gain the benefit of introspection and self-reflection. We can figure out what it is we really want in life—and then we can go out and do it.

6. **Goals Help Us Live Life to the Fullest**—When you take the time to set goals, you ensure that your life is geared toward getting the most out of every moment. That doesn't mean you have to have every moment of your life planned out. At least a little serendipity is good. Like a vacation, you'll find lots of interesting things to see and do that you never would have thought of before you started. Your destination might change as you travel down the road and learn more about yourself and the world you inhabit.

What's critical to know is that you can change your goals—they are *your* goals—and you *should* be flexible and open to changing or creating new ones as you assess your progress toward a goal or new interests emerge. The goals need to be realistic, part of the accurate self-assessment, but they need to contain inherent short- and long-term "ambitions" so that you are pulling yourself toward the things you seek to achieve in your life and career. Reaching small goals leads to big accomplishments over time.

If you're in college, your goals could be to get an internship this summer, to meet three people who are working in areas of interest/passion to you within the next month, to become involved in one or more extracurricular activities in your department or university, and/or to participate in a study-abroad program. If you're starting a career, a goal could be to get coffee/lunch every two weeks with someone working in a desired position or field, to practice mixing/editing, or to write for an hour every day.

Your goals should not be confined strictly to career achievements. They might also involve improved nutrition or health, better relationships with family and friends, or contributions to others in terms of time and/or money. These types of goals are also important because they nurture the career goals you seek. If, for instance, you are not eating nutritiously, you will not likely have the energy and, perhaps, drive to consistently follow through on more career-specific goals. If relationships with people close to you are not as good as they should be, your "support structures" might hinder to some degree your ongoing development and career-related aims. You want, as best as possible, to use all areas and resources in your life to be in positive concert with where you want to go. You'll be better off in the long run.

There are any number of goal-setting approaches or programs you can access online. This chapter is not meant to be a full-blown goal-setting seminar, but rather to impress upon you the importance of setting—and *writing down*—specific goals to help service your larger ambitions. One of the most commonly used is "SMART" goal setting. SMART is the acronym for:

Specific—What is the specific goal you're trying to accomplish? Be SPECIFIC!

Measurable—How can you measure your success? How will you know when you've accomplished the goal.

Actionable: What are the action steps (aka objectives—your plan) needed to achieve the goal? Break into smaller steps. List every step.

Responsible/Relevance: Who are the people that must support this goal? Do you need the support of someone else (manager, coworkers, friends, or family)? Why is it meaningful to your career?

Time-bound: When do you want to achieve the goal?

Let's say you want to get an internship during the upcoming summer.

Specific Goal: Earn a Summer 20__ Internship at a _____ company (in location(s))

Measure: Receive two or more internship offers

Actions/Achievable:

1. Create a tip-top resume (and cover letter as needed) attuned to *each* position applied to by (date)
2. Make a list of people you know that might be resources for internships (e.g., professional contacts; a peer who has interned where you'd like to intern; someone you know that knows someone working in the industry) by (date)
3. Create a list of companies offering an internship and/or companies you would want to intern for by (date); check at least once a week for any new internship opportunities
4. Apply to a minimum of ten internships by (date)

   a. Apply for *two* additional internships for each one "rejected"

5. Follow up with each (where possible) within one week after listed application deadline
6. Interview with two or more companies

Responsible/Relevance: Gain experience in a professional setting; make connections and build relationships with contacts; learn what I need to work on; make better distinctions about what I do and don't want to do

Time-Bound: Receive offers by May 15; begin internship on/before June 1

This takes some time and practice, but setting goals will help you focus on what's important to you in ways that will save time in the long run and, more practically, increase the odds that you will have success getting what you want.

The same process can be undertaken with critical relationship-building (discussed in the next attribute), development of specific hard and soft skills, and specific knowledge you need for your career. Remember, your goals are *your* goals, consistent with your interests (passions), values, and aspirations. They *will* likely change as you age, gain experience, and encounter new opportunities. Embrace this reality because, when applied, it will lead to amazing things that you *can't* visualize! That's a very cool thing!

Final Word about Your Ambition

Your ambitions and goals should motivate you to work hard and smart, pay attention, connect, and persist toward your goals. In concert with your ethical values, work for what you want with an eye toward eventually finding a career you're so passionate about that doesn't feel like work *to you*. If you don't put in the time, it's merely a dream. If it's a true ambition, you'll wake up ready to tackle your goals each day with positive energy. Take comfort that you will utilize the 12 Attributes of Extraordinary Media Professionals to ever-greater effect. The resulting outcomes will be amazing, if not always fully predictable, in The Big Picture.

AMBITION Exercises

1. What is *your* definition of success?

2. Describe your "Dream Job." Then answer the following:

   a. What type of work would you be doing on a daily basis?
   b. What is your work environment (or culture) like?
   c. Name a person who is doing now what you would love to be doing in the future.
   d. Based on your "Dream Job," what do you see as your *first/next* job?

3. Make a list of five media/career professionals whose careers you would like to emulate. What appeals to you about those people and/or careers? What do you know (or believe) are the key reasons that explain the successes they've achieved?

4. Career goal setting

   Create a list of long-term goals connected to your career. These should be subdivided into three time frames: Big Picture (ten or more years), five years, and one year. Think in terms of positions, skills, and knowledge connected to your career aspirations.

   Then, using "SMART" goal-setting strategy (or similar), write out shorter-term goals for each, breaking into six-month, three-month, one-month, and one-week goals. Make a daily to-do list to work toward your short- and long-term goals.

5. Repeat the aforementioned process for at least three of the following areas that are relevant to you:

   (a) Financial, (b) Education, (c) Family, (d) Artistic, (e) Attitude, (f) Physical, (g) Nutrition, (h) Hobby, or (i) Public Service.

Part II

The Active Attributes

Characterized by energetic work, motion, progress or participation

[P]eople who end up with the good jobs are the proactive ones who are solutions to problems, not problems themselves, who seize the initiative to do whatever is necessary, consistent with correct principles, to get the job done.[1]

We typically associate the word "proactive" with "initiative" or acting in anticipation of future problems, needs, or changes. We know it's a positive trait to have. What you may not know is that proactive personality is tied to an array of objective and subjective success outcomes. Proactive people make more money, are more satisfied with their career ("happy"; like their jobs), and gain greater access to resources and opportunities than those who are not—or less—proactive. Proactive personality also significantly influences the success of job searches, including those of recent college graduates.[2]

Being proactive is considered beneficial for all occupations, but perhaps few more so than the media and creative industries. In fact, media professions essentially *require* that you are proactive in approach. There are simply too many uncertain career-related variables—work-related challenges, high competition, and technical/business changes—to enter into them *hoping* to be successful or to "catch a break." Too many people want to do what you're doing, even when what you're currently doing seems uninspiring to you.

Big Picture attributes are important, but not sufficient, without effective application of Active Attributes. You must serve as your own *agent* in your own personal and professional pursuits: taking action, paying attention, building relationships, and persevering (at times), all while remaining true to your own values. When you consistently and effectively enact upon your environment good things—often *very good* things—will happen. Trust in that.

Interestingly, proactive personality is considered by most a "dispositional" quality, meaning either we are born with it or we aren't (we "have it" or we don't). Is this actually true? I do believe there are human tendencies that lead one to be relatively more or less proactive. However, I believe greater levels of proactivity are possible through application and habit. The simple knowledge of its importance toward career success—especially for the media professions—should be a motivator to become more proactive. You really have no other choice.

Those who master the Active Attributes—Connective, Resourceful, and Persistent—will be *self-leaders* oriented to *pre-act*. You will effectively (and creatively) solve and anticipate problems (Resourceful). You will consistently take steps to build a network of *meaningful*, lasting personal and professional relationships (Connective). You will have the wherewithal to keep pushing past any and all obstacles, especially when no one is looking or pushing you to do so (Persistent). The successful activation of these attributes will help make you top of mind *to others*. Over time, your proactive approach will lead to more money, more career satisfaction, and will be aligned with your aspirations, helping you gain access to key people and resources that lead to even more opportunities.

Connective

The ability to develop relationships and attract opportunities

Synonyms: Interact, Ally, Unite, Join, Attach, Network, Affiliate

Antonyms: Separate, Sever, Detach, Divorce

Surround yourself with people who have dreams, desire, and ambition; they will help you push for and realise your own.

—Law of Attraction

A few years ago, I had the great honor of meeting Grant Tinker, the legendary founder of MTM Productions and later president of NBC. I had read countless articles in which creative professionals admired Mr. Tinker's leadership style and skills, showing uncommon admiration and loyalty for this long-time executive. I was intrigued as to why creative people gushed about this "suit" in such glowing terms when most suits are viewed by creatives as the "enemy."

Then retired, Mr. Tinker (my gushing admiration won't allow me to call him "Grant") welcomed me into his beautiful high-rise apartment on Wilshire Blvd. in LA. I had an entire list of questions ready to ask and had promised not to take too much of his time. Though I was ready to fire away with my questions, Mr. Tinker promptly began asking about *me*: where I was from; where I went to college; what I studied; my career path; my research and teaching interests. He showed curiosity about *my* story, seemingly far less interested in telling me what he knew. Although this might have been the smoothest of techniques, Mr. Tinker's manner and approach seemed anything but that.

It quickly became quite apparent why some of the most successful creatives voiced such high admiration for Grant Tinker. He *listened* and was genuinely curious about people and their stories. Because he effortlessly and naturally came from that place, he created bonds with colleagues and was able to make better, more informed decisions involving them, which only deepened those connections and the mutual trust that resulted from this level of interaction.

In that short two-and-a-half-hour meeting (it flew by—and was supposed to last no more than ninety minutes), I was able to ask better questions because it wasn't Q&A, but instead a *conversation* that generated deeper, more insightful answers.

Being Connective: Building a Network of Meaningful Relationships

"Networking" probably doesn't evoke the fondest of images, and perhaps you think of it as a necessary task (or evil) in the process of developing a career in media. My notion of "networking" is to be in a room—perhaps at a party or some media industry social gathering—with twenty-five or fifty or more people. Everyone is circulating: shaking hands, chatting, and exchanging business cards. People I know do this with extreme effectiveness and genuine ease. My hat's off to them (and I'm a little envious), because I'm not a natural "mingler." It feels uncomfortable to me personally, although I've gotten better at it. I would much rather be off at a table in an intimate, yet animated, conversation with only two or three people for the entire evening. These larger networking occasions do occur and you may likely be in those situations from time to time, but I'm happy to state that these smaller-scale interactions constitute the bulk of activities that could be counted as "networking."

I tend to avoid the term "networking," because it feels calculating and impersonal, as if we're engaging with people with the sole purpose of getting something *from* them. While this difference might be more semantic than real (and reveals my own values/biases), many young or aspiring professionals seem to recoil (at least slightly) from that word. I'm happy to know most people feel that way because our personal contacts and relationships should mean more than attempts for personal advancement. In practice, what we might visualize as "networking" should be one small component of a bigger and, ultimately, more enriching process.

I prefer the word *Connective* because it not only encompasses the ability to communicate and network but also is a way of thinking about how we should interact with others. Being connective is more than being a good speaker or writer, or having the courage to glad-hand colleagues at a social function. Relationship-building is a conscious effort that is nonetheless organically derived through the attributes discussed—YOU, Passion, Ambition—and also manifest through active attributes as well those that help your career endure. The key for you is to develop a *network of meaningful relationships*, which will be of paramount importance to your career—and to your life.

CONNECTIVE CLICHÉS TO TAKE TO HEART

A good attitude gets you everywhere.
The little things can mean everything.
You have two ears and one mouth (listen at least twice as much as you talk).
Never burn a bridge—EVER!
Your reputation precedes you.
It's a (shockingly) small world.

Just like any meaningful relationship in your life (a parent, spouse, partner, sibling, friend), the depth of the relationship is built over time. You can't expect someone to trust you immediately, nor should you expect the people you meet to immediately give you the levels of trust required to gain access to coveted projects, titles, and resources. It's a process (a word you've already heard a lot and will again) to be undertaken and also *enjoyed*. Viktor Frankl states that success, like happiness, must *ensue* (*not* a pursuit). So, too, is being connective.

So, the Connective attribute is *much* more than networking. Connective means that you are *attracting* a group of people and relationships that are *mutually* beneficial. You give as much or more than you take. There is a certain depth to the connections—or at least to the key ones—that leads people to either want to work with you or have a desire to help you succeed. In competitive, collaborative, nonlinear media professions heavily populated with strivers, the ability to be "top of mind" is critical to a successful, long-lasting career.

"It's Who You Know" Is Only One Part of the Equation

In almost every type of business you'll hear, "It's who you know," implying (rather negatively) that you must have some connection or "in" in order to secure a job or opportunity. The deeper implication is that qualifications matter less than having the "right" contact. Eve Honthaner's *Hollywood Drive* adds to this phrase with "It's Who You Know *and Who Knows You.*"[1] This is a significant idea because if other people don't know who you are—if you haven't made an impression or impact on someone through your work or relationship—they are not likely to select you when opportunities arise.

I've added what I believe is another key part to this phrase: "It's Who You Know and Who Knows You *for the Right Reasons.*" You want to be top of mind with others for positive reasons, not negative ones. Negative reputations are remembered just as vividly as positive ones (if not more so). If your reputation is bad with someone, your opportunities to work with that person probably are, too. Just as significantly, due to the inherently social nature of media professions, your reputation (good and bad) will extend beyond your immediate connections.

ATTRIBUTE TIP FOR CAREER SUCCESS

Be Great at "The Good Hang"

In LA, "The Good Hang" is a term assigned to people who not only are highly competent but also have a great attitude and are able to keep things light and positive during long days of collaboration. These are the people who are asked back to work on future projects and build connections without overtly trying to impress. It's simple: people want to work with people they enjoy being around as long as they are competent.

My mentor once told me before my first job interviews, "If someone goes to the time and trouble to interview you, you are qualified for the job. They now just want to see if they want to be around you." This is one of the best pieces of advice I've ever received and I've since witnessed this play out during numerous interviews and work-related interactions.

You want to be the person others see themselves *wanting* to work with. You give yourself important advantages by developing a network of *quality* connections—people who can vouch for your work ethic and performance, as well as your Good Hang.

As you might guess, I believe "It's Who You Know and Who Knows You for the Right Reasons" is how it *should* be! This doesn't imply that unqualified people should be selected over highly qualified people. But why should someone hire an applicant that perhaps looks good on paper (a resume) over an applicant whose work they already know or who comes by reference from someone else they know and trust? Yes, nepotism happens, too, and might prove extremely frustrating to witness in specific circumstances (e.g., when you're up for a job, and someone you believe is clearly less qualified than you is selected—or even worse, a clearly unqualified family member). Through your own connective actions, you, too, over time will *earn* your advantages toward opportunities and advancement that might, to others, seem unfair. You'll know you earned these opportunities because you've connected with people in a highly effective way.

Take Emily Shkoukani as an example. Emily was a student in the LA program I run. Emily was a quiet and unassuming leader. During the program, Emily landed two internships and her evaluations were excellent. Each internship emphasized Emily's genuine personality, her work ethic, her reliability, not to mention the high quality of her work. One of the internships even continued to employ Emily to do "coverage" (i.e., critique scripts) after she returned to Ohio. I also saw these qualities on consistent display throughout our LA program. Emily engaged during class and interacted effectively with professionals. Simply put, Emily made our LA program (and me by extension) look good. Over time, I came to know Emily as an extraordinary person with an outstanding future.

One more thing about Emily: She has an unyielding passion for everything *Star Wars*. This was well known to our group, especially as Episode 7 of *Star Wars* was to be released at the end of our fall semester. Upon returning to Ohio, Emily decided to apply for an internship the following summer at Lucasfilm in San Francisco and asked me to provide feedback on her resume and cover letter. I knew an alum who works at Lucasfilm and told Emily that after her resume/cover letter were ready, I would send it along to my contact and put in a good word for her.

But that's not exactly true. I put in a *great* word for Emily with my contact, expressing with enthusiasm and confidence the person I knew her to be. Here's what I wrote in my email to our alum (omitting name):

Hi—,
I wanted to briefly see if I could get your insights or advice . . .
One of the LA program students, Emily Shkoukani, is applying for a Story
   Development Internship at Lucasfilm. Emily is truly top-notch—she had

two development internships in LA last Fall (continues to do coverage for one of the companies), works hard and smart, is great to be around, and loves Lucasfilm/*Star Wars*. Is there any advice or specific contact that might help enhance Emily's opportunity for this internship?
I'm very careful about asking for these things, but believe that Emily would be an exceptional intern.

Here's the response I received:

Hey Roger—I forwarded your email on to the story coordinator at Lucasfilm. Not sure if the position has been filled or not, but that should at least help move her resume higher in the pile!

As you might guess, Emily eventually got the internship at Lucasfilm (after three interviews). Emily didn't get this opportunity *because* of me or my contact. She got it because of her great qualities and experiences, a resume and cover letter that were attuned to the position, and her ability to communicate who she is (which included a deep love of *Star Wars*) during the interviews. But the connections helped without a doubt. More important, the ways in which Emily was *connective* (through her genuine personality and work) helped her land the internship (which, by the way, eventually led to a full-time position at Lucasfilm).

Hiring for a position is *not* an objective process. There are some variables in your control (e.g., having a tip-top resume/cover letter that's well organized, persuasive, and attuned to the position; who you might know) and a lot not in your control (e.g., who applies, who someone knows). Those who connect well gain advantages that increase the odds for positive outcomes. Securing a job or an opportunity often involves a "third person": someone you know well that knows someone well that you don't know. When an opportunity arises, what will the person say about you to the other person that might give you an inside track for the opportunity?

Connective is the "central nervous system" of the 12 Attributes Model because it *vitally* serves most, if not all, attributes in the model. People want to work with people they know and trust—or come on recommendations from people they know and trust—and will often choose someone who is great to be around over someone wildly talented but difficult to work with. You want people to *want* to help you, and you do this by giving people *reasons* to want to help you—through your hard work, your passion, your ability to be a solution, your willingness to see things through, your adaptability and reliability. As you build your network of relationships effectively, as people can vouch for your talents and ability to work well with people, opportunities will emerge. Trust the process. Know that relationships *matter deeply*, especially in media professions. Great relationships lead you to expand your network and will open opportunities you might not even be aware of. Strive mindfully, yet genuinely, for meaningful relationships both in and out of the industry. (Also know that as you become successful, you'll take great pleasure in helping those you see with similar qualities.)

Emily's example is only one and perhaps not the norm. Oftentimes in media and creative professions, individuals work on a contract or freelance basis and move from job to job. Who are the people who *get* those jobs? *How* do they get those jobs? It's almost always through someone who knows them already or is referenced by a close contact that knows you and the person hiring the position. "Every job I've gotten came from someone I've known or worked with," said Michelle Gritzer, a successful assistant director in LA. I've heard those very words from countless media professionals.

You want to be the "top of mind" person that others think of first when an appropriate opportunity comes up. Through your work and personality you are *known* to be good at what someone needs. You can be relied upon and are pleasant to be around (which helps on long days). Countless professionals have told me that they will hire an "A person" (i.e., someone who is great to be around) with "B talent" (very competent) over an "A talent" (highest competency) who is an "F person" (someone who is difficult and/or has a negative attitude).

ATTRIBUTE TIP FOR CAREER SUCCESS

Be Nice to EVERYone (Especially the Gatekeeper)

Because the media world is so shockingly small, you will be surprised by who knows who, who has crossed paths with whom, and how someone you know can connect you with someone "they" know. This is very important to keep in mind at all times. The last thing you want to happen is to be cut off from a potential opportunity because you weren't nice to, or were dismissive of, someone. So, be nice to *EVERY*one!

A common mistake people make is dismissing the power of a gatekeeper—a company's receptionist/secretary, personal assistant, or PA. The gatekeeper is often the first person you will talk with on the phone or while sitting in the reception area waiting for that interview or pitch meeting. Gatekeepers control access to decision makers. Unfortunately, some treat the gatekeeper as "low level," overlooking their genuine power. This is just plain stupid to do. Especially as a young or aspiring professional, whose first job will likely be beneath your education level—and quite likely similar to the position you're dismissing—the presumption of any superiority or entitlement is the quickest way to be shut down.

I'm told that after an interview the boss will often casually ask the gatekeeper, "So, what do you think [of the person just interviewed]?" Why is this? The boss trusts the opinion of the gatekeeper, who also observed you when you weren't as "on." The gatekeeper might have as good or better sense of how you will be in a work environment than a boss who is speaking with you in a more formal context.

Even more critically, gatekeepers in the media professions are themselves usually *strivers* with goals of advancement. They may be a key connection as you and they move up in a profession. So, be nice to EVERYone, because today's PA or office secretary might be tomorrow's development executive, producer, news director, recording engineer, or internship supervisor.

Brian Unger, who was on the first iteration of *The Daily Show* and later the host of *How the States Got Their Shapes*, once told me one of the most impactful things I've ever heard about the media and entertainment professions. "You have to come to terms with the randomness of this industry," Brian told me. "Things I've thought were sure bets fell through at the last moment, and things I didn't even know were in the works just seemed to fall in my lap. If you try to make sense of it all, it can drive you crazy."

One of the most important ways to help reduce the uncertainty and unpredictability of these professions is to maintain and build important relationships. Things more often seem to "fall in your lap" when buttressed through great work and excellent relationships that are working for you (even when you don't know it's happening). Simply put, the better the depth and breadth of your relationship network, the more likely opportunities will fall your way. Be mindful of this.

"Gratitude changed my life," said writer/filmmaker David Alan Hall. "It attracted other people who helped me build personal relationships and a professional network."[2] The most connective people are often the ones that feel the "luckiest" in their successes. They marvel at how things "fell their way" in their career and how someone gave them an opportunity that seemed unwarranted or unearned at the time. This doesn't happen by accident, and it happens to performers like Brian Unger and to more introverted successes like Emily Shkoukani.

The power of being connective can be so compelling that (ironically) as your relationships deepen in the industry and you prove yourself through your work, you may scarcely need a resume (but have one ready), because people will already know about you and your work and the job will largely be yours before you're interviewed (if there's an interview at all).

As they say, your reputation precedes you (both good and bad). These outcomes are a result of your work, how you conduct yourself while at work, and the ever-deepening connections that result from these efforts. Because media and entertainment industries are public and collaborative and so many people get jobs because of who they know and who knows them (for the right reasons), you'll find that the world within which you work is shockingly small. People know people or know "of" people in ways that are hard to fathom. The old "Six Degrees of Kevin Bacon" seemingly needs only three degrees of connection within the media professions.

Simple, Yet Powerful, Ways to Be Connective

Being connective involves a complex mix of activities, interactions, and situations that combine to build connections and relationships over time. There's no single way to do it and the myriad of personalities (and personality types) make this a dynamic process to say the least. However, the things you can do to be connective in your job or internship are often quite simple. The following are some of the ways to help build your relationship network.

Work hard and smart. So simple, right? People take note of those who arrive early, stay late, and work hard all day. Perhaps more important, people tend to *invest* in those that demonstrate a consistent ability to work smart: take initiative, solve and prevent problems, and anticipate needs. Working hard and smart is a natural relationship builder.

Stay in touch with connections you make. Because life gets busy, we all can fall into the trap of not staying in touch with people like we should. Don't let the meaningful connections "dry up." Develop strategies to stay in touch. I'm often asked "how" one can stay in touch that doesn't feel awkward or forced. Some of these are quite simple, such as a birthday message on Facebook or a Christmas card; others require you to pay attention to people's deeper interests. Send your boss/colleague a link to an industry trade article that you think might be of interest to him or her. They might or might not actually click the link and read the article, but they'll remember that *you* sent it to them. If, for example, you know of someone's deep allegiance to a sports team or a favorite hobby, send a quick email or link related to the interest as a way to stay in touch. Find ways to stay connected with your best relationships that can be both fun and genuine. Be that person who consistently stays in touch (without being a nuisance, of course), and you'll be remembered for all of the right reasons!

Do the little things (they mean a LOT). Building strong connections is not generally manifest via grand, expansive gestures, but more often through small, yet meaningful-in-the-moment gifts of time or work—or actual gifts. The simple *offer* to stay an extra fifteen minutes so that someone can finish a project (or be able to go home without something lingering over them) might be of surprising significance to a boss or coworker (remembered by that person months or years after you've forgotten about it). It's amazing how something that is small/easy for *you* to do will make a big impact on someone else. The most valued resource for successful professionals is their *time* (or lack of). If, in your internship/job, you can make someone else's time *easier, better, shorter*—even in the simplest ways—you will become valued. Great relationships are often built from doing the little things.

Send handwritten "thank you" notes. After an interview, completion of a job, a significant interaction, or when someone does something meaningful for you, follow up soon after with a "thank you" note. Emails are good, but handwritten notes are *gold!* So few people actually do this that you'll stand out (maybe less after this book, but still worth the effort)! Purchase a box of small thank you cards and be in the habit of following up with a thank you. In special circumstances, get creative by sending something you know they would value along with the note. Bring in donuts on the last day of your internship (*always* a winner), and drop thank you notes in their mailbox.

Pay careful attention to details. The most consistent "negative" I hear about early career professionals (and interns) is not paying careful attention to details. Making unnecessary, careless mistakes (e.g., not proofreading) costs time, creates frustration, reduces trust, and can cost money. If you are great at attention to detail, you'll develop *connective leverage* for yourself and enhance your relationships because you will prove to be reliable. Do every task/responsibility correctly the first time. If you don't fully understand what is needed/expected, don't be afraid to ask the person how it should be done. Colleagues will appreciate your desire to do it right. Then make sure to do it right.

Look to give as much as you take. Building connections, for some at least, feels mercenary or calculating. This is *not* the way to think of the relationships you seek to build. "Relationship" implies a deeper connection that, on some level, binds people of similar interests, values, and goals. This doesn't mean you don't seek something *from* the relationship, but rather that you carry a perspective of seeking to give *to* the relationship as well. What we give can be quite simple and intangible (e.g., time, patience, empathy) or more tangible (donation, opportunity). Some relationships will be stronger than others, but maintain a perspective of "giving" as well as "getting."

Be yourself. There is a fair amount of ego, fakery, and bluster in the media professions, and your radar will need to be up, but ultimately you will make more and better connections when you are your most genuine self (i.e., *YOU*). Over time and in the majority of situations, your uniqueness and genuineness will connect you with people who are most important to your career and life. Bonds are much stronger and longer-lasting when they come from a genuine place.

Make Every Interaction Meaningful: Learning and Listening as a Pathway to Connecting

To close discussion of the Connective attribute, I want to share a vital piece of advice that I give to every student and young professional working in the industry: Make every interaction meaningful. What do I mean by this?

Every time you interact with someone—and this means *every*one—make that moment important. *Be in the moment.* Seek to connect with them. Be curious. Ask questions. Smile. Look them in the eye. Listen. It sounds so simple, perhaps a little silly or unrealistic, but if you develop this as a consistent habit, you *will* connect.

Pensado's Place creator and cohost Herb Trawick offers a great piece of advice, with a touch of admonishment, for how technology too often plays to our detriment in the media professions, especially when relationships and connections matter so much.

"Lift your head out of your phone," Trawick says. "Don't be the head-down society. If I'm in a meeting with you, I need to know what's in your head. You need to be able to process. As we say on the show, 'don't let technology use you, you use technology.' It's an incredible asset, but if you're stuck to it, can't function without it, take a break from it."

"I'm going to hire you based on how you relate to me," Trawick continues, "not how quickly you scroll to find information. If you don't learn to network and know how to connect, you'll never get to the top. This is the difference between how champions get selected vs. those that get left behind."

People connect with people who have a thirst to learn and grow, have a genuine curiosity about people and processes, and have their eyes up and ears open. Most people mistakenly think that education is finished upon graduation from college. In reality, your education in the industry is only beginning. You may not be working strictly within your area of passion, especially early in your career. But you can always display a passion to learn and grow. You should have enthusiasm about being in professions that continually encourage you to develop yourself in such a myriad of ways. And you will, at times, learn what *not* to do—or how *not* to be. These are sometimes the most powerful, impactful lessons of all.

I believe the most underrated communication tool is *listening*. We think of "communication" as *expression* (our thoughts, feelings, perspectives, perceptions), but an equally powerful form of communication is the art of listening *genuinely*. You'll not only learn more by listening but also connect with people when they believe you are genuinely interested. And you'll be better at your work because you're attuning your activities accurately to what occurs in any work or social situation. You'll ask better, more resonant questions. You'll be more *connected* to the environment around you, which in turn will allow you to be more effective in your relationships and work. This is becoming a lost art as devices (e.g., mobile phones) lead us to have our eyes and head down too much of the time.

Think of someone you know that you consider to be a great, genuine listener (a close friend, parent, boss). What's going on? What tells you that they're a great listener? Are they asking you questions? Do they show a curiosity about you, what you've done, what you know, where you've been, where you want to go? How do you *feel* about this person? How does this person make *you* feel? The easy guess is that you feel very positive about that person. You have a respect for, and bond with, that person. That's how I felt during my brief, but impactful, interaction with Grant Tinker.

Connections are built on the work you do, how you go about it, and the attitude you bring to tasks and projects big and small. People do take note of your ability to connect effectively and this has an impact on the short- and long-term opportunities presented to you. This is why people with strong connections often get work or opportunities that seem to come from nowhere. Their ability to make a positive difference in any circumstance helps form the connections that bind people together and lead to additional opportunities of distinction. The simple day-to-day habits and approaches you take make an impact on others.

CONNECTIVE Exercises

1. List three of your very best relationships: (ideally) a family member, a friend, and a coworker/boss. What tells you each relationship is "special"? How do they differ from each other? Be specific.
2. "Getting Coffee" is a code phrase in the media industry for meeting and getting to know someone in an informal way.

   a. Select a current media professional that you would like to meet and schedule a meeting (ideally in person, but virtually is good, too; do this when it works best for your source and this could also wind up being lunch/dinner, tour of the office, etc.).
   b. Soon after the meeting, send a short, concise "thank you" note (preferably handwritten), expressing your appreciation for the person's time and insights.
   c. Repeat (a) and (b) at least every two weeks.

3. Select three people in the media professions that you particularly admire or hold in high regard. If you were to meet them, what would you want

to know to gain insights about their success? Make a list of five key questions you would ask.

4. Create a spreadsheet with current (and aspiring) media professionals in your relationship network. Provide columns for (1) name; (2) email; (3) phone number; (4) current position/company; (5) relevant info (hobbies, past projects/companies); and (6) last contacted. Create additional relevant columns as you see fit. Develop a strategy to stay in consistent contact with your relationship network. Continually update your relationship map as your network expands.

Resourceful

The ability to act effectively or imaginatively

Synonyms: Enterprising, Industrious, Self-Starting, Clever, Inventive, Shrewd
Antonyms: Unimaginative, Content, Complacent, Inert, Lazy

> It's not the lack of resources that causes failure, it's the lack of resourcefulness that causes failure.
>
> —Tony Robbins

In his first week as an office PA, Terrell Boaz was asked to assist the casting director. Terrell soon noticed what frustrated his boss most about her job: dealing with the hundreds of emails she received that day. "She was so unhappy and a lot of it stemmed from an unending stream of emails that wouldn't relent," Terrell says.

On day 2, Terrell came in an hour early, logged into the casting email for the show his boss was in charge of, and went through every email—more than 200—that had been received since the previous day. Terrell proceeded to type up one giant email for his boss that was a summary of all the casting highlights: name, age, race, gender, and how good he thought they would be on a television show. He sent this to her email account.

"She showed up at 9, she sits down and opens her email," Terrell recounts. "She looks at me and said, 'What the f— did you do!?!'"

Terrell panicked. "I am *so* sorry. I saw how much frustration the emails gave you and how much pain it was causing you and I thought this might help."

The new boss leaned over, hugged Terrell, and said, "What are your hours?" Terrell said he worked 9 to 9. "She said, 'hold on.'"

"She gets up, walks to the other side of the office," Terrell recalls. "You literally hear some screaming, and she comes back and says, 'you work from 10 to 6 now.'"

"I said, 'What?' She said, 'now you're my casting coordinator.' I'm like, 'no, this is not how it's supposed to work. I've never worked in casting before.'"

"She said, 'I don't care. I like you, and I'm keeping you, and you're getting a raise.'"

"And, I'm like 'alright! Here we go!'"

Be the Solution

We tend to think of creativity—or being creative—as "dreaming up" an idea, story, innovation, or concept. We also tend to think of success as a product of pure talent and inspiration. But another "talent" is perhaps even more important to your career: being a *resourceful problem-solver*. As Terrell's example illustrates, when you use your imagination to *act* toward personal, collaborative, and/or organization benefit, you are exercising an incredibly powerful attribute that can have a significant impact on your career.

The most valuable resource to successful media professionals is NOT money or title or a big house or an expensive car. The most valuable, coveted resource is *time*. As Chris Rock said, when you have a career there's never enough time. Our time is limited, all the more so for driven, successful people. You'll understand this even more as you become more and more successful, but it's an important concept to take to heart *now*.

Early in your career, you will most likely be assisting someone else, working for someone (e.g., a "boss"), or otherwise doing a lot for/with a little (especially money). But if you can make your time and the time of others *better*, *easier*, and/or *shorter*, you will soon gain value for yourself and within your relationship network. As Stephen Covey writes in his classic *The 7 Habits of Highly Effective People*, "The ones who get jobs are the proactive ones that are solutions to problems, not problems themselves."[1] Your resourcefulness will be key to getting jobs and will serve as an important leverage-builder to eventually gain access to resources within your profession.

ATTRIBUTE TIP FOR CAREER SUCCESS

Commit Simple Acts of Resourcefulness

Annie Hunnel was one of the three students sent to work a *Monday Night Football* game when it came to Dallas. As a "runner," her role was basically to assist with anything that needed to be done during the telecast. She came recommended by a professor who had come to know Annie as a highly reliable student. *His* reputation was on the line if he wanted to provide future opportunities to students, and her reputation was great. So he recommended Annie.

Upon Annie's arrival to the production truck at the stadium a few hours before kickoff, the lead producer of the broadcast told her, "Wait right here. I've got something to take care of, and when I get back I'll have something for you to do." The lead producer exited the truck. Annie soon noticed that several computers were still in boxes. She promptly took the computers out and set them up.

Upon re-entering the production truck, the producer said, "Oh, could you hook up the computers?"

Annie motioned back toward the computers, "I already set them up," she replied.

Such a small act to perform. Such a *big* impression was made.

Annie continued her great work. Toward the end of the game, Annie was asked if she could work in Pittsburgh in a couple of weeks. She did and was then asked to work the Super Bowl. Annie's act of resourcefulness opened the door for new, unanticipated opportunities.

Simple acts of initiative can lead to significant impressions. Offer to stay an extra fifteen minutes to help someone finish a task at the end of the day. Arrive early so that your boss can start his or her day on the best possible foot. Look for ways to show that you're a solution. Colleagues and employers like people who work hard but *value* people who work *smart*.

A significant amount of work in the media professions involves some form of problem-solving—meeting deadlines, finding financing (or making a lot out of a little), resolving a technology issue on the fly (or learning a new one), securing a location (or finding another one last second), hiring/firing people, and many, many more. Those with an ability to consistently "figure it out" enjoy tremendous advantages and often advance more quickly. Maybe not as quickly as Terrell, but when you are solution-oriented you make things better for others, and that makes things better for you over time.

Extraordinary media professionals *act* upon their environment rather than react to situations and problems. As a young or aspiring media professional, what you have to offer is your mind, what is uniquely you, and the energy of youth to attack problems and be solution-oriented. This attribute rests beside Connective because being an effective problem-solver makes you a natural connector to others. Your resourcefulness, connected to your passions and desire to continually learn and willingness to adapt and persist, brings with it positive energy that organically attracts you to other successful people and organizations. Moreover, research shows that resourceful people are not only better at achieving their goals but also respond better under stress because they focus on "solution" rather than "problem."

Think of being "resourceful" as more than a mental skill; it requires the ability to process information emotionally as well. Terrell *felt* how the overwhelming number of emails impacted the emotional well-being of his new boss, and he quickly took action to relieve/release this problem. The boss was *moved* to not only hug him but also march across the office and demand that he be promoted. Your resourcefulness can *literally* move people!

The 80/20 Rule × 2

There seem to be a lot of "80/20 rules"[2] in our world. For problem-solving, spending 80 percent of your time on the solution and no more than 20 percent on the problem is a very good rule of thumb. The 20 percent is important because you need time to accurately identify what the problem is so that you're in the best position to effectively solve it. You might also need the 20 percent to allow yourself time to feel bad or upset in order to "get past" the issue so that you can turn your focus toward the solution.

As a graduate student, I worked on a series of research projects with my advisor and mentor, W. James (Jim) Potter. When we received reviews from journal editors about a manuscript we had submitted, Jim would read aloud each review and the research team would spend a few minutes absorbing, often grousing, about the comments from each reviewer (most comments were constructive, some made no sense). We had worked many hours collecting data and writing our manuscript, so we felt *emotionally* attached to our work.

After he finished reading the reviews, Jim would literally clap his hands and say, "Okay, what do we need to do to fix this?" It was at that point that we focused on addressing and resolving the issues cited by the reviewers. This approach led to a successful outcome (i.e., publication) *every* time.

But the effect of being solution-oriented can be even more powerful than simply being good at solving problems over time. People who are best at "solutions" become conditioned to take initiative and *anticipate* problems (known or unknown) before they even occur. This creates its own 80/20 rule, because the most effective problem-solvers prevent 80 percent of problems from becoming "problems" in the first place. Using the previous example, as a writer I became better at anticipating *potential* problems (reviewer comments), which gave me the power to address real or perceived issues up front, and resolve many—but not all—of the issues before they even came up. When you are proactively working to prevent problems before they occur, you are setting yourself up for exponentially better results because you have additional time and energy to focus on other things, including the problems that do come up.

Think about it. Do you know people who are the *opposite* of the 80/20 rule? They spend 80 percent of their time on the problem instead of the solution or, even worse, spend *100 percent* on the problem and wallow in it—never doing anything about it. They become mired in an endless loop of dwelling/talking about the problem, but little time actually doing anything to resolve it. Are these people going to attract people and resources to gain opportunities in the short and long terms? Do they carry positive energy? You know the answer.

But do you also know people who are *looked to* as great solutions, trusted to resolve almost any problem or issue. Would you rather have this person on your team or the wallower? Which of the two do you think will attract more opportunities and breed more successful outcomes over time? Which will have more people saying good things about them to others? The answer should be clear.

Be one of those people.

Make Constraint Your Friend

Robert Rodriguez attained legendary status for making *El Mariachi*, his first feature film, for a "whopping" $7,000. On his DVD commentary for *El Mariachi*, Rodriguez stressed the need for cost cutting at every turn, "because if you start to spend, you cannot stop anymore." So, what are some things Rodriguez did to cut costs and yet make a movie that looks like it cost a lot more than $7,000?

* He did not use a slate—actors signaled the number of scene and number of take with their fingers.
* He did not use a dolly—he held the camera while being pushed around in a wheelchair.
* He shot the film without sound and then recorded on-set audio so it could be synced in post-production.
* No film crew was hired; actors not in scenes helped out.
* Scenes were filmed sequentially in one long take with a single camera but every few seconds he froze the action so he could change the camera angle to make it appear that he used multiple angles.

*He shot the opening shootout using the actual female warden and male guard to save the costs of hiring actors and renting clothing.

*He shot on sixteen-millimeter film as opposed to thirty-five millimeter and transferred the film to video for editing, avoiding costs of cutting on film.

Originally, *El Mariachi* was intended to be sold to the Latino video market but was rejected by straight-to-video distributors. Rodriguez then sent his film (cut as a trailer at the time) to bigger distribution companies, where it got attention. Companies invested to improve the sound quality and market the film. Eventually, *El Mariachi* won the Audience Award at the 1993 Sundance Film Festival and an extraordinary career was launched.

And by the way, Rodriguez raised about half of his budget by participating in experimental clinical drug testing while living in Austin, Texas.

The budget for *El Mariachi* was originally $9,000, so he actually came in $2,000 *under* budget. *El Mariachi* made $2 million at the box office.

Rodriguez was resourceful in his approach every step of the way, and the outcome was better, more interesting, more creative, more memorable. Over time, he gained access to more resources through his resourcefulness and continues to enjoy the benefits of his approach to filmmaking.[3]

LESSONS ABOUT CREATIVITY FROM ROBERT RODRIGUEZ[4]

1. Do see obstacles as opportunities to be creative.
2. Don't underestimate the value of loyalty.
3. Do focus on things you're passionate about.
4. Don't be afraid to delegate.
5. Do relax; you can still get plenty of work done.
6. Don't worry about failure; it's the key to success.
7. Don't do something just because that's how it's always been done.

In reality, few of us ever have carte blanche in terms of resources to do what we want, when we want, however we want.

And that's a good thing!

"The enemy of art is the absence of limitations," the great film director Orson Welles once famously said. Going even back further in history, Michelangelo said, "Art lives on constraint and dies of freedom." The director of *Citizen Kane* and the artist who created the statue of David did not create these great works of enduring art due to the absence of restrictions, but *because* of them.

There is a famous story attributed to Ernest Hemingway, who supposedly bet friends that he could write an entire story in just six words. Seems difficult, if not outright impossible, right? Here's the story Hemingway wrote:

For sale: baby shoes, never worn.

What thoughts and images come to your mind through this six-word story? We don't know all the details of this story, but it's a story nevertheless and a compelling one at that. Hemingway proved how you can not only tell a story via constraints but also perhaps tell a more powerful story *because* of the constraint. He had to focus his words, structure each word to make it count, and be highly creative for it to make an impact. This is an important lesson for young and aspiring media professionals.

"Creativity is what happens when a mind encounters an obstacle," says Ben Orlin. "It's the human process of finding a way through, over, around, or beneath. No obstacle, no creativity."

Constraint fosters creativity rather than limits it and enacts your resourcefulness to figure out a way. "Constraints force you to think, they boost brainpower," says Thomas Oppong in his article "For a More Creative Brain, Embrace Constraints." "With constraints, you dedicate your mental energy to acting more resourcefully. When challenged, you figure out new ways to be better. The most successful creative people know that constraints don't limit their efforts . . . they give their minds the impetus to leap higher."[5]

Kara Harshbarger interned as a casting assistant during the production of the film *Paulie*. Her primary responsibility was to look after young star Hallie Kate Eisenberg on set. During that time, Kara wrote a short script about a father/daughter relationship through their mutual love of baseball. Kara, through her amazing personality and work ethic, befriended Eisenberg, her mother, and key crew members on set. She persuaded the camera department to save the film "short ends" (leftover film from each camera package) so she could use them for her production and shoot on thirty-five millimeter and also persuaded some crew of a multimillion-dollar film to work weekends on her short film. Kara, with little experience and almost no money, shot her fifteen-minute short and submitted it to a Lifetime Network "Young Women Filmmakers" competition. *A Little Inside* was one of four films selected. From there, Kara expanded the idea into a feature-length screenplay, raised $1 million, and directed her first feature film.

ATTRIBUTE TIP FOR CAREER SUCCESS

In Business Communication, Less Is Almost Always *Better*

I hate the long email, and I would bet good money you do, too. As a general rule, do you like opening a personal email with long paragraphs and tons of details? Are you typically excited to read it? People in business are busy, and you are generally *not* their priority. You'll receive a quicker, more positive response if you write short, concise, to-the-point (yet well-thought-out) messages.

Say exactly what needs to be said and no more. Make every word count. Writing less actually takes more work because you must consider carefully what you're stating. It's your responsibility to make the communication as clear and concise as possible and not the person you're trying to get access to for their help, time, or a possible job. In business communication, less is almost always better. And that's better for you, too.

As you grow through your successes, take on more responsibilities, and time becomes a more precious factor in your work and leisure life, you'll be even more appreciative of those who communicate in ways that make it worth your time.

Resourceful people, like Kara, then only twenty-three, actively think ahead, work toward goals, creatively figure out ways to make something happen when they might seem impossible to almost everyone else, and then follow through to make it worth everyone's time and effort. They don't think in terms of limitations or what can't be done, but use the constraints to generate energy and focus toward successful outcomes.

For nearly twenty years, my school at Ohio University has held an annual 48-Hour Shootout. It's a very popular event where teams of students have forty-eight hours to conceive, write, shoot, and edit a short film (five minutes or less) to be delivered for screening exactly forty-eight hours after each team draws at random a prop, a line of dialogue, and a genre, which all have to be incorporated into the finished film. These constraints of time (forty-eight hours and five minutes) and imposition of structures (genre, prop, dialogue) often yield amazingly interesting, even inspired, short films. Participants agree that the energy and focus required to pull this off successfully in forty-eight hours play a key role in creating innovative productions, while often providing the additional benefit of *bonding* people together through the intense, time-constrained activity.

An interesting, revealing thing happened during the second Shootout in 2003. A talented team of students randomly drew "Musical" as its genre, a particularly challenging genre to produce in forty-eight hours. The team delivered the film *four minutes* late and was disqualified. Extremely disappointed, yet undeterred, the group took the opportunity of a little extra time to re-edit and "sharpen" the film, and then submitted it to an MTV University Film Competition. The film, *Detonate*, disqualified from the Shootout for being just minutes late, won the national award! This led to an invitation to attend the Sundance Film Festival and internships at MTV.

The group exhibited other key attributes, including Persistence and Resilience, for not giving up and finding a way to turn a negative into a big positive. Yet resourceful thinking—to figure out how to write a story, create and choreograph, shoot, edit, and deliver a musical in forty-eight hours (and four minutes, technically)—and to figure out "somewhere" to send it led to a film that eventually won a national award and created many career opportunities for the team. The constraint focused their creativity, and the group's persistence and resilience further enabled a positive outcome. Now, these professionals work at major studios and are impacting the media industry as writers, producers, casting directors, editors, and more.

"Well, when it comes down to me against a situation, I don't like the situation to win."

"The best way to beat a problem is to make it work for you."

"How can you feel confined when you're in touch with the universe?"

"If this works, it'll keep us from getting caught. If it doesn't, it'll keep us from getting old."

"Remember the episode when I couldn't figure out how to solve a problem using the things I had in hand? Yeah, me neither."

And resourceful wisdom from someone even *smarter than MacGyver:*

"Imagination is more important than knowledge. Knowledge is limited. Imagination encircles the world."

"Try not to become a [person] of success, but rather try to become a [person] of value."

Challenges and constraints tied to your interests are not really holding you back unless you've chosen to see them as a problem. Build important muscles of problem-solving *and* creative thinking that will serve you well in the short and long terms. Embrace the opportunities for creative action that constraints help encourage. They will be among your best friends!

RESOURCEFUL Exercises

1. In *exactly* six words . . .

   a. Tell a story
   b. Describe yourself
   c. Describe your one-, five- and ten-year goals

2. Describe a challenging or difficult situation in which you came up with a creative solution. What were the circumstances behind the situation that helped drive you toward successful solution? What "constraints" (internal or external) were involved (e.g., time, money, or personnel)? What did you learn about yourself that, if it were a habit, would make you a more consistently resourceful person?

3. Within your work environment or specific activity (e.g., job/internship, club, organization), initiate two simple actions that will specifically make someone *else's* time better, easier, or shorter.

4. Describe situations where you feel "paralyzed" by having too much time or too much to do. What strategies can you employ to resourcefully act toward better outcomes?

5. Participate in a competition that is constrained by time (e.g., 48-Hour Shootout) and/or resources. *Note*: If such a competition doesn't exist, *create it* (ideally with others with similar interests)! Creating an event connected to your interests will, in itself, enact your resourceful attribute. You'll have problems to resolve, people to encourage and pitch to, and grow in the process of creating/participating in something that will benefit you and others.

6. There are dozens of websites with hundreds of problem-solving games and activities to help you practice problem-solving and thinking outside the box. Google "Problem-Solving Exercises" and solve at least five of these.

Persistent

Firm or obstinate continuance in a course of action
in spite of difficulty or opposition

Synonyms: Determined, Relentless, Fearless, Constant, Brave, Grit
Antonyms: Fleeting, Temporary, Transient, Intermittent, Inconsistent

If you are home and you are sitting on your couch, all I have to say is that this is hard work. I've worked hard for a long time and it's not about winning. What it's about is not giving up. If you have a dream, fight for it. There's a discipline for passion and it's not about how many times you get rejected or you fall down or are beaten up. It's about how many times you stand up and be brave and keep on going.
—Lady Gaga's Oscar Speech

Walt Disney was down but not out. It was 1928 and the twenty-six-year-old cartoon animator was taking a train back to California after a disastrous trip to New York City. His distributor had just taken over the rights to Disney's first big-time character, Oswald the Lucky Rabbit, hiring away Disney's best animator in the process.

Disney determined to press on despite extreme unfairness and financial hardship.

Although his studio was left unstaffed and in debt, Disney wouldn't admit defeat. Instead, he vowed to start over with what he had—his talent. As the train shot through the Midwest, Disney started doodling on a piece of paper. It wasn't long before Disney thought the doodles looked like a mouse.

"Walt never thought he was beaten at anything—ever," said his wife Lilly in *The Man behind the Magic: The Story of Walt Disney* by Katherine and Richard Greene.[1]

Disney persisted despite—likely *because*—of many other setbacks before and after Oswald the Lucky Rabbit was taken from him, including bankruptcy and a mental breakdown. He explained his formula for overcoming failure: "To some people, I am kind of a Merlin who takes lots of crazy chances, but rarely makes mistakes. I've made some bad ones, but fortunately, the successes have come along fast enough to cover up the mistakes. When you go to bat as many times as I do, you're bound to get a good average."

And, by the way, Walt Disney was rejected *302 times* before he got financing for his dream of creating the happiest place on earth.

"It is good to have a failure while you're young because it teaches you so much," Disney once said. "For one thing it makes you aware that such a thing can happen to anybody, and once you've lived through the worst, you're never quite as vulnerable afterward."

What would the world be like if Walt Disney did not persist, instead wallowing in self-pity and giving up?[2]

Persistence Is *Fuel* for Your Success

The most successful media professionals are acutely aware of how unfair and difficult the industries can be. For example:

Oprah Winfrey was told she was too unattractive to be on TV.

What if she believed the doubters and naysayers and gave up? How different would our world be?

J. K. Rowling was jobless and living off welfare. In 1993, Rowling's marriage ended in divorce and with just three chapters of the Harry Potter saga completed. Two years later, her Harry Potter manuscript was rejected by all twelve major publishers. Rowling persisted, and a year later a small publisher gave her a tiny advance of £1,500 and published just 1,000 copies of her book. Rowling has since sold more than 400 million copies of her Harry Potter books.

What if Rowling had stopped writing?

Steven Spielberg was rejected from the University of Southern California School of Theater, Film and Television three times, and still he didn't give up on education or filmmaking. Thirty-five years and multiple Academy Awards later, he returned to school to finally complete his work and earn his BA.

What if Spielberg didn't reject the rejection?

And what if Lady Gaga didn't show such grit and determination?

The Disneys, Oprahs, Rowlings, Spielbergs, and Lady Gagas of this world obviously didn't succeed because they had it easy with no obstacles in the way. They became extraordinary *because* they encountered challenges that made them stronger, more resolute, more competitive, and more willing to persist even against the highest odds. It made them better. They even came to appreciate the difficulties they overcame because it *amplified* them. They used persistence in the service of their ambitions.

As former senator and professional basketball player Bill Bradley once said, "Ambition is the path to success. Persistence is the vehicle you arrive in."

Now, consider the following realities if you are an aspiring or early career media professional:

—You'll struggle at times in your career, especially early on.
—You'll have setbacks and short-term "failures."
—You'll interact with people who don't believe in you or have your best interests at heart.
—You'll witness others with less "talent" get opportunities or "breaks" when you do not.

What is your reaction to these statements? If you believe they won't apply to you, you're likely both incorrect and unrealistic about your paths to succeed in media professions. You don't have to "like" the previous statements, but it's important to be realistic about what you're getting into if you believe in your passions and ambitions. Things might happen *to* you (e.g., big disappointments and temporary setbacks), but your persistence will provide the fuel to help make extraordinary things happen *for* you over time.

Can we become truly successful, self-actualized people and media professionals without facing *any* challenges or obstacles? Maybe, but I don't really believe so. More to the point, do you really believe it's in your long-term interests to not encounter *any* obstacles, to not face setback and challenges? Consider the following quote from Tal Ben-Shahar, who wrote *Choose the Life You Want*:

> When we hear about extremely successful people, we mostly hear about their great accomplishments—not about the many mistakes they made and the failures they experienced along the way. In fact, most successful people throughout history are also those who have had the most failures. That is no coincidence. People who achieve great feats, no matter what field, understand that failure is not a stumbling block but a stepping-stone on the road to success. There is no success without risk and failure. We often fail to see this truth because the outcome is more visible than the process—we see the final success and not the many failures that led to it.[3]

Persistence is a type of obsessive tendency to push forward—to finish that script, to follow up with a potential employer or a key contact, to keep going after a rejection, or to continue to develop a hard skill when getting to the "next level" is difficult—often when no one cares that you persist. Some people in the media professions succeed simply by sticking it out when many others drop out. Your determination to keep going when things are difficult plays a big role in your ultimate success, as important as innate talent, sheer creativity, or exceedingly high intelligence. The willingness to persist often taps into who you are and what you're really made of, especially for pursuits that truly matter to you.

SEVEN REASONS WHY PERSISTENCE IS THE KEY TO SUCCESS[4]

1. *Persistence makes you an expert*. With persistence, you continue to do the same thing over and over until you achieve success/master the task.
2. *Being persistent will motivate you to try harder*. You'll try again and again. Motivate you to put more effort to get closer to your goals.
3. *Persistence is a sign of being ambitious*. When you keep attempting something with persistence, people around will look at you as an ambitious person.
4. *Persistence will set a good example to your colleagues*. Others will be inspired by your level of persistence and will try to imitate it.

5. *Persistence teaches you the value of success.* As you learn that success is not easy to achieve, you will understand the true value of success. You will become enlightened about the amount of hard work and dedication required to make something happen.

6. *Persistence will help you gain experience.* Going through the process of making mistakes and learning from them, understanding how and why things go wrong, will give you experience that you can't learn in a book.

7. *Persistence will make you aware of your weakness.* Your weaknesses will only be exposed when you analyze your failures and try to find out the things you lack: how and where you need to get better; whose expertise it will be wise to ask for.

As discussed with the Passion attribute, a growth mindset is very useful here because you see your skills and abilities as something you can develop and cultivate over a long period, perhaps your entire life. Persistence does not imply a hard-headedness to the point of not being adaptable or open to change. Instead, according to Dr. Carol Dweck, "In a growth mindset, people believe that their most basic abilities can be developed through dedication and hard work. *This view creates a love of learning and a resilience that is essential for great accomplishment.* Virtually all great people have had these qualities" (emphasis added).[5]

Persistence is a "capacity-builder," like a muscle that becomes stronger through resistance. As you push against and through obstacles, your muscles expand as do your abilities to become better and to make key distinctions about what is important to you. Persistence also is critical to build other important "attribute muscles." Your willingness to persist increases your confidence, thickens your skin (Resilience), and connects with people more likely to devote time on your behalf when they see that you're "in it to win it" for the long haul. Persistence fuels your ambitions and clarifies what you're *truly* passionate about. It builds your character and shines more light on who you really are. You will become more resourceful in approach, able to adapt as needed to get what—and where—you want. You'll be unafraid to fail and *use* the fear of failure to your own benefit.

There's an adage in screenwriting that applies so precisely to life itself: you can tell more about a character by what they *do* than by what they "say." This means that more is revealed by action than words. Persistent people are putting tangible action toward what they want to do, often when no one else is looking or demanding it. This builds your *character.* Take consistent action in the service of your ambitions that can be seen *and felt* by others. Start doing this now.

The ability to persist is particularly important to younger professionals because your initial jobs and responsibilities often aren't in sync with your grander ambitions. So the questions become: What are the types of things with which you persist? What are you willing to "stick with" because they matter to you? What do you *enjoy* when challenged? What brings out your competitive side? And more specific to your career: What are you so enthused about that you won't let obstacles or barriers (real or perceived) get in your way?

ATTRIBUTE TIP FOR CAREER SUCCESS

Be Persistent . . . but Don't Be Annoying

In my own career, I have witnessed many people whom I could clearly call "persistent" but soon came to the conclusion that I would never, *ever* want work with them. Why? They crossed the line from being persistent to being *annoying*. Why would I want to spend eight or more hours a day with someone whom I believe to be annoying? Why, after telling someone I would provide an answer "in one week," would I want to work with someone who contacts me every day to ask about the position? The person *is* being persistent. But this type of persistence leads to *avoidance*.

Generally, media professionals appreciate persistence because they view it as a valuable attribute. Successful media professionals have demonstrated persistence to get where they are. Persistence can be a double-edged sword, however, so be careful and be aware. It's okay to be a "squeaky wheel," but be a *gentle* squeaky wheel when the time is right.

What do you do if you really want that valued job/internship? Follow up in a structured, logical, think-of-the-other-person manner. Ask if it would be okay to follow up, and then be sure to do so. If the company says a decision will be made in one week, follow up eight days later (give them the entire seventh day). Check back a week after that. Don't be upset or take it personally if you haven't been contacted. Business gets busy, and the job/internship you seek might not always be *their* top priority.

Remember, people often hire who they see themselves wanting to be around all day. You want to be one of those people.

"The value of persistence comes from a vision of the future that's so compelling you would give almost anything to make it real," says Thomas Oppong in his article "Persist. It Matters."[6]

You'll discover your true interests by your willingness to work on them. For example, if I'm booking a flight, I will persist to reach a desired outcome because I have a passion for travel and confidence that I can figure it out. If, however, I have a water leak in my house (considering myself as the *least* handy person on earth), my willingness to persist will not be high because I have little interest, inclination, or confidence (or ability) to resolve the issue. In this situation, I won't persist at all. I will simply call someone who is an expert. But I will work hard if the issue, problem, or activity exists in the plane—literally and figuratively—of high interest to me. That's why persistence works most effectively as a product of a passion or an ambition. You're more likely to find reasons to persist and keep going, and you'll become more creative in your approaches to attain a successful outcome.

Persistence puts your personal values and what's meaningful to you *into action*. A lot of people have high ambitions and would "like" to be a successful musician, writer, producer, TV personality, or journalist. Many enjoy the idea of gaining the financial fruits and high-profile notoriety found in one or several public industries. Persistent people put their ambitions on display through commitment and continual effort.

The term "persistence of vision" is another key metaphor, often associated with the projection of film, that suggests the value of being persistent.

Persistence of vision refers to the optical illusion that occurs when visual perception of an object does not cease for some time after the rays of light proceeding from it have ceased to enter the eye (i.e., the continuance of an effect after the cause is removed).[7] Consider what an outstanding metaphor that is for your life and career. As you have "big dreams" to succeed, your willingness to persist within your "vision" will carry beyond what you've done in any specific instance.

The group discussed in the Resourceful attribute, winning a national MTV award, would have never enjoyed the benefits of their resourcefulness had they not persisted despite their initial disappointment with being disqualified. Without persistence, they would have never had the opportunity to reap the rewards that came.

So simple. So many people simply don't follow through or keep going.

Those who "quit" and "give up" and let the disappointments defeat them don't deserve the fruits of their effort, while those who persist through and despite the obstacles have *earned* whatever fruits may follow. Those who persist are winners in the end and look back with pride *because* of the obstacles they overcame.

Persistence and the Multiple Benefits Paradigm

With any difficult or challenging endeavor, rarely does a single benefit provide the amount of motivation needed to carry you through to a successful outcome. If you can understand—and even internalize—*multiple reasons* to undertake any worthwhile challenge, you'll be more willing and able to see yourself through the rough spots that the challenge will inevitably present.

I call this the "Multiple Benefits Paradigm": If you can see *several compelling* reasons to see something through, you'll be able to maintain the motivation necessary to attain a successful outcome. The benefits derived via the Multiple Benefits Paradigm can be tangible (e.g., "I get to travel"; "I get to see my family more often"; "I will develop X skill") or intangible (e.g., "I will grow as a person"; "I will expand my horizons"), and they can come from positive fuel (e.g., "I will be able to provide more for my family") or negative fuel (e.g., "I will prove them wrong"). Use the weight and significance of all reasons for you to *leverage* your pursuit of any worthwhile goal.

Here's a personal example of the Multiple Benefits Paradigm: In 1995, I applied for a Fulbright Fellowship to Japan. I had just returned from my first international trip (to Australia) and was intoxicated by the idea of living in another country. Through this excitement I discovered the Fulbright Program but had less than three weeks until the deadline. A fire was lit within me (like you wouldn't believe!), significantly aided by the Multiple Benefits Paradigm: (1) the opportunity to live in another country for an extended period; (2) the challenge of "making it" in a place where I didn't speak the language; (3) for my family to have a common, yet extraordinary, experience; and (4) for my five- and eight-year-olds to have exposure to a broader world.

Importantly, notice how my drive to achieve this goal fundamentally had very little to do with career advancement, although I understood the benefits there, too, and could add it to the list. But career advancement was no higher than #5 in my own mind. Benefits to my career would be largely *incidental*, not the primary reason for doing it. I simply wanted a way to have an impactful experience, and I had plenty of compelling reasons to put in the effort to make it happen.

I was relatively young and probably not the most qualified on paper. But I connected with the Fulbright officer in DC, getting invaluable feedback on the courses I proposed to teach and on my purpose statement. I continually refined the application to make a compelling case for my selection. I was focused, relentless, and willing to put whatever time and effort necessary to create a successful outcome.

Fortunately, I was selected for a Fulbright Fellowship and my family spent eleven months in Japan. It was wonderful, challenging, and life-changing. A bit of resourcefulness with a strong desire to see it through made all the difference.

But what if I hadn't been selected, as I haven't been for many other things that I wanted? I would have been disappointed, yes. But I submitted the application with a certain comfort that, regardless of the outcome, I had done everything I could to make a compelling case. I would have also used what I learned in the process as *fuel* to make it work the next time around. That fuel would've been added to the list of multiple benefits.

Your persistence is best served when connected to your deepest values and to what motivates you and that has to be determined by you. You're simply not as likely to persist if not in sync with who you are and the (principled) actions you're willing to take in pursuit of any worthwhile goal. If you can't find multiple reasons for doing something worthwhile, then perhaps it's not worthwhile to you.

Too many people get too focused on how. "How" represents the pragmatic parts of our brains. Viktor Frankl is famous for saying, "If you have a big enough *why*, you can almost certainly figure out how."[8] The Multiple Benefits Paradigm helps you focus on *why*, centers you on what your *heart* wants, reduces the influence of the more practical "how," and moves you closer to where (and *who*) you really want to be.

And . . . You'll Be *Thankful* for (Some) Things You *Don't* Get

During a particularly upsetting setback in high school, my dad told me something that really stuck with me: "Some things in life you really want you'll look back on and be glad you didn't get them." We have all had those moments when we desperately wanted a job or opportunity. Then, when we receive a negative decision for that opportunity, it is very disappointing. But if you're learning and applying the lessons life gives you—and believe things happen for a reason—you'll often be very happy or relieved in retrospect for what you didn't get. Here are some real-life examples from a variety of experience levels:

Write a "Thank You" When *Rejected* for a Position

No one likes to hear "no," and rejection is one of the most disliked emotions we have; in fact, we often avoid approaching someone or asking for something altogether simply out of fear of being rejected. What's important to understand is that "no" is not necessarily "no forever," but perhaps "no for now"—and is rarely personal. This is especially important to internalize in the collaborative, competitive, "small-world" nature of the media professions where rejection is commonplace. Ultimately, it's how you *respond* to "no" that matters more than the "no!" itself. This offers an opportunity to show your true character, confidence, and desire to persist in the long term.

When you *don't* get a position or opportunity you interviewed for, *be sure* to send a simple, genuine "thank you" message to the person who "rejected" you (as hard as this might be in the moment). Thank the person (1) for their time, (2) for learning more about the company/position, and (3) that you hope your paths cross again. This person will be impressed with your professionalism (and might even have second thoughts about the decision). Your approach sometimes leads nowhere, but sometimes the person selected doesn't work out or suddenly decides to take a different position (and you'll move up the ladder because you followed up in the way you did). Sometimes the person interviewing will remember you when another position comes up in the company or will know someone else looking for someone. And sometimes your paths will cross again and you'll be remembered for all the right reasons. You've made a connection, and that's a good thing.

And at worst, you will have additional fuel to prove the person wrong for not selecting you.

Studio Executive: I was up for an executive position at HBO about five years ago that I fought tooth and nail to try to get, pulling out all the stops and connections I possibly could. I had to jump through a bunch of hoops and had multiple interviews, and the process dragged on for months and months. After running through their obstacle course for the better part of six months, I was really bummed when I didn't get it. A year or so later, there was a big regime change and a lot of the executives under that regime were let go, so while it was really disappointing at the time, I think I probably dodged a bullet in retrospect!

Assistant Director: Several years ago, I was working with an assistant director (AD) team that got a hit series on ABC. I had been with them long enough that I thought I was for sure going to do the series with them as the Key Second, but unfortunately the producers decided they wanted someone else with more experience, so I didn't get the job. I was very disappointed and nervous because I didn't have many other contacts with people who knew me as a Key Second. Luckily, that summer someone asked me to come day play on a movie called *Scouts vs. Zombies*. It was for a level lower than I had been working, but since I did not have a job coming up, and it was short term, I said yes. Four days of work ended up being the entire movie, because the person I was filling for quit. So I stayed for six weeks. Then that first AD took a liking to me, knowing that I was normally a Key, and asked me to do his next show. So, I ended up on the fourth season of

Veep in Baltimore. There I learned so much more about being a first AD and had some of the best experiences of my career. Without that year on *Veep*, I know for a fact I would not be as good at the job as I am now.

Feature Film Development: I was hating my job because it was so administrative, with no access to creative. I was a receptionist and was seeking any way to get out of the job. I interviewed at Chernin and hit it off interviewing with who would have been my boss—so much so that she mentioned that she loves Skyline Chili (a local Cincinnati food) and I immediately two-day shipped an eight-pack of Skyline Chili to me so that I could give it to her on my first day. That's how confident I was. Well, I was denied the job and devastated. I was getting to a point where I would sit in my car and DREAD going to work. I kept doing my best because you never know what will happen. Two weeks later, I was finally offered a desk. It was in three fields I thought I had no interest in—president's office, legal, and publicity. But, because of it, I learned about all areas of the film industry and I got to travel to Sundance. And it led me to my ultimate dream desk—feature film development. Had it not been for the rejection of the job at Chernin, I would not be where I am now—which is on the path to my dream job, at a company I love, and with eight cans of chili.

Student: Just at the start of this semester, I interviewed for a teaching assistant position for digital post-production (class). I really got along well with the instructor and was thrilled that he asked me to interview. So thrilled that I may have been a bit too dead-set on getting the position and was pretty disappointed when I did not, especially when hearing that when it came down to me or one other person. Only a few days had passed since hearing the news when another opportunity was presented to me: to interview for a job opening for director of podcasts at *The Post* (campus publication). While there weren't too many people in the running for this job, I still felt that it seemed a bit "too good to be true," as the job description seemed like something I'd be perfectly happy doing for free! I ended up getting the position, which I am still ecstatic about.

I believe things happen for a reason . . . even when we don't understand them at the time. Regardless of whether any single opportunity we "want" works out, those that persist will land on their feet, leading to outcomes that aren't always predictable but are "meant to be" in The Big Picture. You *cannot* fail as long as you're learning something, not making the same mistakes repeatedly, and making distinctions about yourself that help make you better. That pursuit, whatever it is, might ultimately take you down new roads and through rocky hills and thick brush, but trust that what ensues will be quite extraordinary over time.

PERSISTENT Exercises

1. Describe an instance where you persisted on a task or goal that proved difficult or even overwhelming at the beginning. How did the "Power of Why" impact how you successfully overcame the challenge?

2. Take one of your written goals (from Ambition attribute) and create a list of "benefits" for seeking this goal. They can be tangible, intangible, and fueled by positive or negative reasons. Describe how the Multiple Benefits Paradigm gives you added leverage to accomplish that goal.

3. Describe a disappointment based on something you wanted *badly* or didn't receive (e.g., job, internship, or election/selection), but now look back and are "happy" and/or relieved you didn't receive it.

4. Find an example of someone in the media professions who has persisted despite overwhelming odds. What can you learn about persistence *and yourself* through this example?

Part III

The Enduring Attributes

To sustain without impairment or yielding

We must be willing to let go of the life we have planned, so as to have the life that is waiting for us.

—E. M. Forster

As a teacher, I have long advocated a "last-job approach" for preparing media professionals. What does this mean? The last-job perspective encourages you to think and act *now* in ways that can help sustain your career over the long haul. Interestingly, by developing key last-job attributes before—or as—you begin your career, you are actually setting up for more success *earlier*, which in turn lays the foundations for even greater successes later on.

The Enduring Attributes are potent because they not only help you get to your destination but also are instrumental in keeping you there. The first two Enduring Attributes—Curiosity and Adaptability—are critical in professions where change and competition are ever-present. The continual thirst to learn, experience, and connect as well as the ability to adapt to ever-shifting work, technology and industry environments is of great relevance. Your Reliability and Integrity are incredibly important because your ability to endure in the media professions is based on your consistent performance and the trust you develop within your relationship network. Your ethical values will enhance your reputation within the media industries and allow you to sleep well at night.

It's important to remember that you will likely start your career in positions beneath your education or intellect—and definitely your aspirations—but your effective use of the Enduring Attributes might help you *accelerate* a little more quickly during the early jobs, make you more ready for these opportunities, and put you on a clearer track toward your ultimate destinations. Just as important, they help ensure that your skills are relevant now and in the long term. You can handle almost anything with consistency, figure out what you don't know, and roll with the (figurative) punches brought by any changes in your work or challenges to your Integrity. As an added bonus, Enduring Attributes serve as a solid foundation to build your Confidence and Resilience to reinforce YOU.

Curiosity

An eager desire to learn and to know

Synonyms: Interest, Inquisitiveness, Thirst for Knowledge, Searching

Antonyms: Disinterest, Indifference, Complacency, Stagnation

I'm hungry for knowledge. The whole thing is to learn every day, to get brighter and brighter. That's what this world is about. You look at someone like Gandhi, and he glowed. Martin Luther King glowed. Muhammad Ali glows. I think that's from being bright all the time, and trying to be brighter.

—Jay-Z

Brian Grazer didn't learn much in college, except how to make good grades. Feeling empty from the experience, Grazer decided that he wanted to meet with a famed professor from his alma mater. He sent the professor letters and called the professor's assistant and got no responses. Finally, Grazer waited outside the professor's classroom, approached him after class, and asked for ten minutes of his time. The professor reluctantly agreed.

Ten minutes of coffee turned into a ninety-minute conversation that proved to be a DM in Brian Grazer's life.

And a lifelong pursuit.

"The experience was so far beyond anything I ever could have imagined in terms of learning, emotional and intellectual growth, wisdom, and some real takeaways with what he was doing with neurolinguistics, which was at its most nascent stage at the time," Grazer recalled of his meeting with the professor. "I felt my value as a person becoming bigger just having spent time with this man."

"And that was the moment I decided to start doing curiosity conversations."

Grazer had just gotten a job as a law clerk at Warner Bros. and decided to meet a new person every day in the movie or television business. He had his pitch ready: "Hi, my name is Brian Grazer. I work at Warner Bros. in business affairs. I'd like to come meet your boss, and I promise you that I do not want a job."

"Everybody said yes," Grazer said. "Not necessarily that day, but I learned that if I kept going and pushing and researching, they'd eventually relent and give me the 10 minutes that I could turn into an hour. These conversations became a discipline. And I learned so, so much."

With the success of his first hit movie, *Splash*, Grazer made a fresh, albeit related, determination. "Now, I'm going to meet everybody outside of show business."

And he's pretty much done just that. The Oscar-winning producer of *A Beautiful Mind* and author of *A Curious Mind: The Secret to a Bigger Life* has engaged with hundreds of successful people from all walks of life, constantly searching for knowledge and understanding to better himself.

"Anybody can have curiosity conversations," Grazer says. "You might not be able to start off with Oprah. You could start with your neighbors across the street. Take the risk. They could just blow you off, but they probably won't. Ask real, genuine, thoughtful questions. If you keep doing that and start creating a constellation of dots in the world you're living in, they'll connect and change your life. They'll offer you opportunities you never thought existed. They'll help you find purpose. They'll increase your level of knowledge. They'll improve your social life, your dating life, your relationship with your kids. All of those things will happen."[1]

Curiosity Is More Important than Intelligence

On the first day of my beginning-level "Business of Media" class, I pose the following question to students on a PowerPoint slide: How important is your *GPA* to getting a job/internship in the media professions?

A. Very Important
B. Important
C. Somewhat Important
D. Not Very Important
E. Not Important at All

About two-thirds of the 200 students will raise hands signaling either B or C. When I reveal the answer as I have clearly observed it within media professions, *E*, the class as a whole is surprised, perhaps even a little doubtful of my assertion.

Then I ask the class how important a *college degree* is to getting a job (and some internships do occur after graduation). The answers here are a little more dispersed along the five choices, likely influenced to some extent by the previous question. In this case, the answer *does* land in the B or C range.

SIX EASY STEPS TO CONDUCT A CURIOSITY CONVERSATION[2]

1. Think of every meeting as the best date the person you're talking to will ever have.
2. Do your research.
3. Add empathy. Think, "What is this person going through in his or her life at this moment? What matters to him or her?"
4. Never ask for anything (other than time). It poisons the purity of the conversation.

5. If you can't resist having an agenda, then say, "I have an agenda." Otherwise, you undermine the process.
6. Pay attention. Always have smart, thoughtful, interested eyes.

So what's going on here? If you're a working media professional, you already know the answer; if you're aspiring and have read the attributes leading up to this one, you probably have a good idea. GPA is generally a weak predictor of success in media professions, and the industries are only interested about what you can *do* and what you have to offer of value. But, at least in the early stages, a college degree indicates to many an *ability to learn* (and to see something to completion) and that carries some value for entry-level positions.

It's important to remember that a media-related major, even a college degree, is *not* required for you to succeed in most media-related jobs. College graduates from *all* disciplines work in the media industries. I personally know highly successful media professionals with degrees in engineering, accounting, history, English, and no college degree at all. Media-related degrees are *not* "professional degrees" like nursing or accounting. They are NOT a ticket to get a job.

But what you do *in the process* of your degree can certainly help.

Let's back up just a bit. The unimportance of your GPA to the industry doesn't imply that you shouldn't care about doing your best or even having a high GPA (you might need that for graduate/law school), but rather that if you believe a high GPA alone gives you some type of advantage or "in" on the job/internship market, you are very mistaken. A high GPA indicates your ability to make good grades. The modest positive correlation between GPA and career success stems from the individual's desire to do well in all areas rather than as a direct indicator of future success.

If, however, your overriding goal is to *learn* and *experience*, your degree—whatever it is—will take care of itself and you'll be better off in the shorter and longer terms. The piece of paper that you rightly receive will be incidental to what you gained in the process. This is why many in the media industry strongly value a liberal arts education, broad knowledge, and fundamental abilities to communicate effectively (writing and verbally), along with other skills. These people are viewed as more *trainable*. Those who are well rounded bring a diverse skill set and this offers value to the media professions.

Corey Poindexter chose this approach as a student. A music production major, Corey took classes in physics so he could better understand acoustics. He elected to take classes in linguistics and health sciences to better understand mouth movements. He even took German to help him have professional working relationships with German microphone manufacturers. None were easy, but the classes were relevant. Corey wasn't overly concerned about his GPA, but he wound up with a good one anyway.

"These classes weren't directly related to audio," Corey now says. "However, by thinking outside of the box about my future career, I was able to study these tangentially related subjects to build skills sets that helped me stand out and excel. Thinking about skills that may help build your career and being curious enough to learn new skills keeps you at the forefront."

Thus, ultimately, your desire to learn is more important that your innate intelligence and knowledge, and *much* more important than your GPA. "Being curious isn't something you get tested on," says Brian Grazer. "It's not a public thing. It's private, and the test is a private thing."

More critically, it's important to understand that your "education" is only in the beginning stages when you enter the media professions. It continues throughout your life. This is a *great* thing, and it's fostered by your ongoing curiosity. The very careers you seek demand it over the long haul.

Media are moving targets. Change is constant and inevitable. Technology, modes of storytelling and their delivery/reception, business practices, and audience/user tastes are fluid. You must be adaptable to it (covered in next attribute), but, more critically, you need curiosity to continually feed your knowledge base and growth, which helps ensure that you're working in concert with your values and true aspirations. As Walt Disney once said, "Curiosity keeps leading us down new paths."

Virtually every media professional we deem as "extraordinary" maintains an avid, abiding curiosity about our world and how it works: people, processes, stories, experiences. They are internally motivated to know and experience more. They are in a better position to "draw from" their interactions with ideas and, in the process, often make connections that matter in the short and/or long term.

"It seems that whenever I get curious about a topic, I learn something (or have an experience while learning it) that emerges in a script, sometimes years later," says Emmy-winning writer Dan O'Shannon. "If I weren't curious about different subjects, all my writing would come from a pretty narrow pencil."

"As an example, I was once stuck for an ending to an episode of *Modern Family* ('The Last Walt'). Out of nowhere, I remembered a line I'd read 15 years earlier in a book about the NASA moon landings. That unexpected historical footnote gave me the perfect ending to my story."

ATTRIBUTE TIP FOR CAREER SUCCESS

Have a Hobby/Interest UNconnected to Your Career

I often hear this advice from media professionals: do something that gets you away from your career and the day-to-day grind. It's easy to fall into a trap where your career consumes you and comes at the expense of doing other things you enjoy. This is particularly common in media professions. So, find something of interest to you. This could be anything from a church group, a running club, mountain climbing, a sport, cooking, or any of an almost infinite number of things to give you a respite from the many hours you spend at your job or on your career. This activity can be solitary—it's your decision—but all the better if you can do something different with others who hold a similar interest unconnected to your career.

You'll not only feel refreshed but sometimes inadvertently make a connection or learn of an opportunity that enhances your career in some way. These are some of the very best connections you can make because they started with a common interest unconnected to your specific career.

When I'm working in LA, I attend Kansas City Chiefs watch parties at Jalepeno Pete's in Studio City. More than 100 people congregate every week to watch games together on a big screen. Our common bond is obvious: a love for the Chiefs and, for some, a community of Midwest connections in LA. Some work in the entertainment industry, some don't. Simple chats before the game or during timeouts have led to internships for my students and amazing guest speakers in my classes.

Don't approach this outside interest to "get" something connected to your career, but it never hurts to have your eyes and ears open in case a moment of serendipity happens.

Additionally, media professionals with abundant curiosity function with their eyes and ears open, thriving on experiences. Some of their curiosities are aimed toward professional pursuits, but some have no direct connection. People exhibiting curiosity *connect* powerfully with others and the broader world.

Gretchen Kessler had an abiding interest in traveling the world, especially Europe. During her camera internship at a "very local" TV station in Wales, Gretchen made it known that she was also "open to learning" editing. "Very quickly I was going out on a shoot, filming everything by myself with just the presenter next to me, and coming back to edit the segment to air later that night," Gretchen says.

"Having to hold all the creative information in my head indirectly taught me directing, and after a while I told the station manager that I had an idea for a show, and could I take one of the other camera techs out and film it? He said, 'Sure, go for it. If it's terrible we won't run it, but by all means go and try.' And that's how I became an American 'TV personality' on Welsh television for a few months!"

Now living in Hungary with dual citizenship, Gretchen sought to make new friends upon arriving in Budapest. "I met someone at a party when I was brand new here who said, 'You have an interesting voice, do you like to sing?' And I thought, 'well why not?' So I joined this random Hungarian choir on a total whim and my choir asked whether I thought I could film a music video for them. I knew that I knew how to plan it, film it with all the appropriate coverage, and edit it at the end. All because I decided it might be cool to learn editing while interning in Wales. And, now those choir videos are reaching 40k views on YouTube!"

We all love the idea of focus—and our culture strongly encourages it—and that's important to see projects and goals through to completion (like a college degree). But in the larger scheme of life and career, the ability to see the broader picture, to at times combine diverse ideas into something fresh or innovative, is of incredible personal and professional value.

"A lot of people in our industry haven't had very diverse experiences," Apple founder Steve Jobs once said. "So they don't have enough dots to connect, and they end up with very linear solutions without a broad perspective on the problem. The broader one's understanding of the human experience, the better design we will have."[3]

"Disney's greatest pleasure was in seeing new things and talking to interesting people," writer Bob Greene said. "Whether he was chatting with a scientist or a street sweeper, he asked question after probing question until he had some idea how they did their jobs. Even though his grammar, spelling, and pronunciation were often poor, many people remarked that Disney was one of the most educated men they ever met."[4]

Think of the opposite. If you don't feel like you have anything more to learn, you're probably mistaken. If you think you're the smartest person in the room, you might be in the wrong room. If you're not really interested in learning, are you really that interes*ting*? Are your life's pursuits really your passion if you don't have an interest to know more, to make connections with people and ideas, and to continually expand your knowledge base in industries that *require* this?

Curiosity Is a Special Type of IQ

There are plenty of smart, intelligent people in the media professions. But our curiosity can offer something more profound. According to Kidd and Hayden, curiosity is a special type of information seeking distinguished by the fact it's *internally motivated*—an internal drive to know. A person can have a high IQ without being curious. But a person with curiosity becomes more intelligent in important ways, along with added benefits of increasing perseverance, deeper engagement and relationships, better performance and achievement, and more meaningful goals.[5]

But even more than that, curiosity represents a level of mind and *emotional* involvement that distinguishes those who may "know" certain things and those who seek to know more about a lot of things. "You can't separate intellect and feelings in the work of the mind," says educator Eleanor Duckworth. "Deep learning is playful and frustrating and joyful and discouraging and exciting and sociable and private all at the same time, which is what makes it great."[6]

So, in the bigger picture of life and career, it's not about your Intelligence Quotient; it's about your InQuisitiveness. But we have a fight on our hands: an anti-curiosity culture that encourages us to "know what we need to know" (e.g., for a test). Like Brian Grazer, we must proactively employ strategies to foster our curiosity in the service of our intellectual and emotional growth.

Having (or regaining) a sense of curiosity and wonder is important to your success: "We've moved out of the industrial era and into the information era. Curiosity is a fundamental piece of that work and a powerful tool," says Kathy Taberner, cofounder of the Institute of Curiosity, a leadership coaching team that focuses on curiosity.[7]

Author Daniel Pink takes it one step further, arguing that we've now moved from the information age to the *conceptual age*. Machines and technology can now handle any number of tasks required in our world, except the ability to generate fresh ideas, make connections, inquire about things that do not yet exist, and provide *empathy*.[8]

When we ask "why," it becomes clear how our imaginations must work to solve the problems at hand and create solutions. Our curiosity remains an essential component in our conceptual world and it's important to maintain despite the forces that discourage critical thought and InQuisitiveness.

EIGHT HABITS OF CURIOUS PEOPLE[9]

1. THEY LISTEN WITHOUT JUDGMENT.

Curious people have no hidden agenda. They seek to understand the perspectives of others and are willing to sit in ambiguity, open and curious without being invested in the outcome.

2. THEY ASK LOTS OF QUESTIONS.

Curious people ask questions that start with "how," "what," "when," "where," and "why." They stay away from questions that can be answered with a yes or no.

3. THEY SEEK SURPRISE.

Curious people welcome surprise in their lives. They try new foods, talk to a stranger, or ask a question they've never asked before.

4. THEY'RE FULLY PRESENT.

Curious people turn off their phones and focus on conversations.

5. THEY'RE WILLING TO BE WRONG.

The ability to shelve a sense of being right in favor of being open to the insights and opinions and a broader array of options of others is a trait of curious people.

6. THEY MAKE TIME FOR CURIOSITY.

Set aside time each month to think into the future or pursue something of interest.

7. THEY AREN'T AFRAID TO SAY, "I DON'T KNOW."

Curious people are always seeking new knowledge by engaging in conversations. When asked a question, they aren't afraid to admit when they don't have an answer. It's more important to learn than to look smart.

8. THEY DON'T LET PAST HURTS AFFECT THEIR FUTURE.

Don't stop being curious about new experiences at the expense of being focused on understanding what we've already been through, especially if painful in some way.

Think of something you have a deep passion or curiosity about? Do you seek out additional information about the topic? Do you tend to remember and comprehend it more effectively and efficiently? Are you excited to know more? Are you as likely to "give up" when you hit a bump in the road? Note how curiosity is tied to the other important attributes described in this book. Our curiosity keeps us going and sustains us.

As simple and silly (and nerdy) as it might sound, the process of selecting definitions, synonyms and antonyms for each attribute was one of the most pleasurable parts of writing this book. I just love seeing what words are used to describe other words and how that leads me to new words (or their opposite). My discovery of the definition for passion (an irrational, yet irresistible, desire to do something) was particularly thrilling to me because it communicated exactly what a career in media professions may seem like to you (and others). The overall pursuit of knowledge and understanding is more important that the actual outcome, but getting the "right" or "best" answer is pretty cool, too.

ATTRIBUTE TIP FOR CAREER SUCCESS

Always Have Questions to Ask—Especially at the End of an Interview

The best interviews, especially for media positions, feel like *conversations* rather than interrogations. Always have questions ready to ask based on research you've done on the company or people you're meeting with, but also *listen* closely for even better questions to emerge during the interview/conversation. Your ability to engage with spontaneity enhances your likelihood of a successful interview and for getting the position—or at least leaving a positive impression that might benefit you down the road.

Virtually every interview, even those that feel like great conversations, will end with "So, do you have any (other) questions?" An answer of "No, I don't have any," usually ends the interview on a less-than-successful note. Instead, you might say, "You've answered a lot of my questions, but I'm curious to know . . ."

If all of your planned questions are answered, it's smart to have one or two good "hip pocket" questions ready. The most obvious and simple: "Tell me a little more about your own career path." (Remember, people like to tell their stories.) But there are others. I once suggested that a student ask the interviewer what she likes most about working at the company. The student later texted me, "She was like, 'Wow, no one's ever asked me that. That's a good one!'" That's a "good one" because it asked the interviewer to reflect in a thoughtful way on the positives of working at the company (something she probably doesn't do in the day-to-day grind) and allows the interviewee to gain insight into whether the company is a good one to work for.

The student got the internship.

Ultimately, your ongoing curiosity will lead you to higher creativity, more engagement, and better problem-solving. While some of us think we might want to do one thing, our *long-term* development is often aided by some breadth and variety of experiences. Working on a variety of productions, within a variety of organizations, assuming various roles, and learning how to be a leader *and* a follower, builds important capacities to learn and grow in important ways. The things that might seem irrelevant in one job, or a general curiosity that you are willing to express at an opportune moment, can become highly relevant, even life altering, in unanticipated ways.

"In my interview with Disney, they asked me what my professional goals are," says Andrew Cooke. "I said I wanted to learn [character] rigging [for animation] at some point. [Up until that point, t]he entire interview had been audio related, and rigging was just something I was somewhat interested in at the time. And that was how this audio guy became a rigger. Now I'm one of the head riggers, and I wouldn't have it any other way."

Our pathways, as tech consultant Natalie Fratto says, are more interesting when we're willing to wander.[10]

How Curiosity Works in the Trenches

The concept of curiosity, while of critical importance to your enduring success, can seem a bit abstract or even esoteric in application. So, here are a few examples of how curiosity plays out within the careers of various media professionals:

Audience Intern. Asking to take part in a certain project or even asking to shadow another department/colleague shows that you are willing to learn, no matter what the task. When I shadowed the talent department at the *Late Late Show*, not only did I get closer to the staff and make new connections, but I also got to see the show in a whole new light and it even got me interested in the talent industry, which is something I hadn't even considered in my future career choice!

Production Sound Mixer. So often I've been curious to see what something (dialogue and effects) would sound like with a certain mic, on a certain mount, in a certain position. That curiosity has led to knowledge through the whole experience. . . . I know from past experiments that micing cars for dialogue sound great with a plant in the visor and lav mic on the actor. But, what if I plant a 50 down low? I learn from that curiosity which ultimately helps my mixes sound better.

Journalist. Curiosity has brought to me my biggest and most interesting stories. Many serious stories, of course, like filing a public records request, asking for the personnel file of a local police officer to find out her disciplinary background [which led me] to find out much more than I bargained for about failures of the department. But also amusing/quirky ones, like my call to a school district to find out the age range for participants in a spelling bee, which led the district to realize the winner was too young to be allowed, and the spelling bee to be negated and redone. Asking questions is the only way to get answers.

Writer. I was fortunate to spend two years at *Los Angeles Magazine*, and I'd say almost all of the good writing I did there involved engaging with my own curiosity about the city. What I learned along the way was that taking a deeper look at the places and moments that Angelenos held in common revealed invisible bonds between us, and there is a hunger for that feeling of community and that which we can all share. If you're curious, other people are, too, and if you can find where your curiosity meets theirs, you will do everyone, particularly those who feel isolated, a great service.

Editor. Most of my curiosity is driven by my passion for what I do. It's helped my career by pushing me toward moving outside my comfort zone and investing my time in people who have the same interest. I've gotten a lot of my jobs by being curious on how I could move forward and learning new (editing) programs that could benefit me later.

Radio Account Executive. Curiosity is a huge asset on the sales side of broadcasting. An inquisitive nature is helpful to uncover hidden (or not-so-hidden) objections that would otherwise be a barrier to closing the sale. It's easy for a prospective advertiser to just say "no," but getting them talking about their business and the challenges they face opens a lot of doors that you can then reposition as marketing solutions. Formulating the right questions also uncovers the necessary information that's critical in developing strong creative—this, of course, becomes the driver of the call to action for the listening/viewing public to purchase the advertisers product or service.

Reality TV Producer. When I was a story associate producer (AP) working in post, I was really curious about how things worked in the field. I saw the footage that came back, and heard snippets of stories from the field producers, and really wanted to know what it was like [to be out in the field]. I expressed my desire for field experience to the showrunner and when his field AP left for another position, he pulled me into the field for several episodes. So many producers work in either field OR post, but gaining experience in both multiplied the number of future positions I was qualified for. At the time the other post AP kind of expressed a bit of, "well why do you get to go, I want to go," but they hadn't told anyone or expressed that curiosity before. So the lesson there is that the squeaky wheel gets the oil! Tell people what you're curious about!

As you can see, gaining access to opportunities isn't about having all of the answers, but rather about asking the right questions, having the courage to ask them, testing your ideas out in the world, and a willingness to express your interests to others. Regardless of whether these interests or job tasks are general or more specific in orientation, your curiosity will foster opportunities for growth that will serve you well.

Think of your curiosity as a drive state like hunger, but the hunger to learn. Thus, if passion and ambition serve as your "big-picture fuels" to succeed, curiosity is the food and water that keeps you nourished and sustained throughout your career, allowing you to fully develop critical muscles that foster your long-term successes.

CURIOSITY Exercises

1. Make a list of topics (at least five) that *naturally* arouse your curiosity (media- and non-media-related). Under each, list three questions/statements about the topic that would lead you to gain more relevant knowledge/insight about that topic.

2. Make a list of three *great* questions you would ask the following:

   —A favorite teacher
   —A five-year-old
   —A parent
   —Your best friend
   —The person you most admire in the media professions
   —Two professions *not* directly connected to media professions (e.g., physician, attorney, engineer, pilot, and so on)

   How do the questions differ/vary between each person? What insights do you expect to gain that will benefit you?

3. In your internship or job, find time (when appropriate) to shadow colleagues on other teams or in other departments. What are you learning about these jobs? Do some appeal to you more than others? How does what you're learning/observing provide insights to your core interests/responsibilities?

4. Arrange "Curiosity Conversations" with people inside and outside your core interests. Make this an ongoing "discipline/habit" to broaden your curiosity and understanding.

   Your own interests and curiosities should guide the specific questions you ask, but here are a few to consider:

   a. How did you get started in the industry?
   b. What advice would you give to an aspiring/young professional about building a successful career?
   c. What do you love most about what you do? What are the biggest challenges/obstacles?
   d. What are your hobbies?
   e. What would surprise me about what you do? (What most surprised you when you entered the profession?)
   f. Where do you see yourself in five years?
   g. What are the biggest changes you've seen in your field—and the people who work in them?
   h. What qualities/attributes tell you that someone will be successful?
   i. Who is someone you admire? Why?

5. Read what the pros read! Locate key media industry trade resources related to your interests and make a habit of reading them on a regular basis. Make note of the following:

   —What trends are occurring?
   —Who are the key "players" and decision makers?
   —What technologies or practices are influencing the creation and delivery of content?

Adaptability

The ability to change or be changed to fit changed circumstances

Synonyms: Flexible, Open Minded, Versatile, Adjustable, Well Rounded

Antonyms: Rigid, Unsuited, Incompatible, Intractable

We cannot direct the wind, but we can adjust the sails.
—Dolly Parton

Jessica was given a relatively simple, mundane project to edit that should've been easy to complete. But, like many parts of the creative process, things became a little more complicated than expected.

"We had captured a time lapse of a camping van being built and it was not great footage," she recalls. "Tons of movement and not as many angles as we thought we had captured."

Attempts at reframing and stabilizing the time lapse helped some, but the team was ready to scrap all of the footage, which would've been a waste of time and money.

Jessica then had an idea. "I brought up having the time lapse be just PART of the final asset, following it up with some b-roll of the finished product," she said. "We weren't sure if it would work, but we ended up delivering it and using it as an asset.

"It ended up being the highest performing asset for that campaign! What a shock to me!!! Now, with every flop that comes my way, I'll look at it and say, 'what can we add or take away to make this work?'

"Adapt to a new way of thinking and it could open doors you didn't even know were there!"

Darwin's theory of evolution stated that the best predictor of survival was not a species' intelligence or physical strength but its ability to adapt to changes in its immediate surroundings.[1] Media professionals are quick to second Darwin's theory. In a survey I conducted with nearly 1,200 media professionals, "adaptability" was the *highest rated* among forty-two attributes assessed and also ranked first regardless of gender, age/experience, job type, or education level.[2]

So how and why is adaptability so vital in the media professions, perhaps even more so than many other types of careers? I know of no better way to explain it than through the perspectives of working media professionals of various types and experience levels, particularly through the lens of COVID-19 (which forced us all to adapt). Let's jump in and hear from the pros:

Freelance Producer. I've found that adaptability is the essence of the gig economy. During COVID, I discovered that my broad liberal arts and storytelling background positioned me to bounce around to numerous creative positions and I am so grateful for it. . . . Careers today, especially in creative freelance fields, require constant re-evaluation and the ability to change and reposition. I don't think my job will ever stay the exact same for more than six months at a time.

Journalist. Adaptability is a means of survival. Whether we're pushed to develop new ways to tell stories, take on further responsibilities due to layoffs or other factors, adaptability is the key. I mean, we're literally bound by an Associated Press Stylebook, considered a journalistic bible, that's released every year with new modifications to the craft. In the end, adaptability makes you a less disposable and more versatile storyteller in a newsroom.

Assistant Director. In the business of film and television, the only true constant is change. Being adaptable is the most important quality not only for an AD, but also for a prop master, a costume designer, a production designer, a director, a writer, a cinematographer, and a producer. Without the ability to adapt and change when things go wrong (or even right, but didn't turn out how you had hoped), we would never have any movies or TV shows at all.

Production Company Owner. I think being adaptable is the only way to survive what's coming. . . . I run a production company that makes wine and tourism videos. Throw in COVID that prevents people from traveling and shuts down more businesses. I'm constantly trying to adapt to the situation and pitching new video and content ideas to companies that are struggling to bring customers back. During COVID, I've had to adapt from shooting high-end videos and commercials to helping people set up and stream virtual wine tastings from their phones. I've had to edit iPhone videos and zoom sessions for clients. Budgets have been slashed and you have to go with the flow. Adaptability is the key.

Editor. Adaptability is paramount in my opinion. Whether it's being flexible while on a gig in terms of schedule and duties or being able to create in a wide variety of styles. Similarly, being able to switch between and, in some cases, learn different software on the fly is a valuable skill for a video and photo editor like myself.

Media Technologist. I've found that people I work with that can't adapt or even just accept change really aren't helping anyone. Being in tech, we change *all* the time. Tons of restructuring, priority and roadmap shifts. We're basically still operating like a startup, and personally I think it's great. I truly believe that when you're comfortable you're not growing. And if we were doing the same thing every day for the rest of our lives . . . how boring would that be!?

Production Assistant. Adaptability creates more room for opportunity. A great example is what many of us are going through right now. I have been working as a part of COVID teams on different sets since the industry started again. Being able to step outside of that comfort zone and take on new challenges is essential not only in this scenario but in many aspects of everyday life.

Music Producer. Adaptability helps you roll with the punches, especially within the music industry. You almost have to be a chameleon of sorts while also staying true to yourself depending on what project you're working on. Right now I'm remotely working with a hip-hop label in Chicago while also collaborating on rock music remotely with other people . . . two different genres! You have to be able to adapt to the different flow, lifestyles, and sounds of those around you to succeed.

Freelance Producer. I've found that adaptability gets you more work down the line. I've had quite a few projects that had very last-minute asks in regard to changing labor and scope of work, and every time my team has been able to make it happen. Not only that, but we do it well. This led to the client continuing to ask us to do the work, rather than going to another team. . . . It takes a certain level of skill and knowledge to be able to adapt to changes in scope on the fly, and each time you have to make those last minute changes, you learn something new. This then leads to you being more prepared for a change on a later project. So skill begets adaptability, which begets skill, which begets . . . on and on. Changes are a challenge, and if you're good, you learn from challenges.

Influencer. Adaptability is important within a job or career because we are all servicing somebody. There are customers and there are colleagues. At all times when we clock in (sometimes when we aren't), someone may be counting on you no matter how minuscule. . . . Adaptability can be more of a gained skill and that's what makes it important, but I'm looking at it more so as why do others need you to adapt and why does a job care that you do. . . . You can't adapt if you aren't learning and paying attention.

Music Licenser. Adaptability is the key at my company. We are a newer team (three years old) processing more royalty and copyright requests in less time and in a new system, all the while working from home due to COVID-19. If I had not adapted, I would be stagnant or obsolete. Since I have adapted, I am now managing a twenty-person team and guiding how we adapt to the various challenges we face.

Junior Creative Executive. The art of communication is something I'm constantly learning about and finding new ways to do. There are different ways I communicate notes to various partners; there are different ways I communicate to various teams within the company; there are different ways I communicate to individual people on my team. But this also goes both ways, because just as I had to master different ways to communicate to people, I also had to learn all the ways those people communicated *back* to me. And truthfully, this isn't something I've concretely mastered because there will always be new projects, new partners, and new people. It's something I constantly have to adapt and change with, but it certainly has become easier over time.

Editor. In every job I feel like there is a certain level of expectation when it comes to adaptability. As an assistant editor, I have had to teach myself new things that no one on my team knows how to do, and my teammates have had to do that as well. Working in a field that forces you to be adaptable is truly a win for all parties involved. By constantly learning, you are benefiting the whole team and sparking new conversations where there weren't any before. Questioning the "how" on a daily basis is important in the media industry! If there is a more efficient way of doing something, why aren't we doing it? When you have to adapt to a new way of doing something (take working from home as an example), you learn new ways to communicate and are forced to enhance your workflows and processes and figure out how to get from point A to point B while keeping up with quality of work that you usually produce.

Production Assistant. I started at the absolute bottom of the food chain as a part-time, third-shift PA. That's a fancy way to say I printed scripts and ran them from the third floor to first floor. And run back up and down with physical paper changes. One of the most invisible members. Becoming adaptable and rolling with the changes—and rolling with a good attitude—grabbed the attention of my senior team members. Soon, my name is on the top of the promotion list. My boss at the time credits the adaptability I brought to the team as a main reason I was able to be noticed! When asked for one piece of advice I always say—be adaptable.

As we can readily see, media professionals in various fields view the ability to adapt as a critical conduit to opportunity, to growth, to advancement, and to building meaningful relationships. With adaptability, you're better able to manage, even *thrive*, in an uncertain, sometimes uncontrollable, world of changing environments. Without the ability or willingness to adapt, we are susceptible to being "stuck" or irrelevant altogether. Those who are rigid in approach and inflexible not only experience more difficulties within the job but also miss out on important opportunities to grow and advance in the profession.

FOURTEEN SIGNS OF AN ADAPTABLE PERSON[3]

Adaptable people

1. experiment,
2. see opportunity where others see failure,
3. are resourceful,
4. think ahead,
5. don't whine,
6. talk to themselves (but not in a weird way),
7. don't blame,
8. don't claim fame,
9. are curious,
10. adapt (duh),
11. stay current,
12. see systems (the forest, not just the trees),
13. open their minds, and
14. know what they stand for.

Research consistently supports the impactful benefits of adaptability. Career adaptability correlates positively with finding work and advancement. Rudolph, Lavignne, and Zacher analyzed ninety research studies focused on career adaptability and found it to be significantly associated with an array of positive subjective and objective outcomes, including cognitive ability, self-esteem, proactive personality, optimism, satisfaction, organizational commitment, employability, promotability, income, lower job stress, entrepreneurial outcomes, and life satisfaction. Those who are adaptable experience improved relationships, have higher levels of performance, make smoother transitions between work roles, are more effective leaders, and even exhibit better mental health.[4] It's easy to see how adaptability can impact all stages of a career, including the early career challenges highlighted throughout this book.

This is why those who succeed the most are those best able to adapt to changes in their environment and may also help illuminate why "Intelligent" ranked *twenty-fourth* among the forty-two attributes as assessed by media professionals.[5] A certain level of cognitive ability is obviously important, but your ability to learn and grow—and adapt—is even more so. As physicist Stephen Hawking once said, "Intelligence is the ability to adapt to change."

It should be extremely apparent by now: media are always changing and evolving—technologies, audience tastes, work roles, and business practices. Collaborative by nature, you must work with others, with a variety of personality types, sometimes competing interests, and often rely on the expertise of others to help accomplish your own work. Sometimes you're a leader, and sometimes, even when you're in charge, you're forced to be a follower (we can't be experts at everything or always do everything at once). Things go wrong: technology doesn't work, people suddenly don't show up, a coworker/boss is a total jerk or incompetent, or you don't agree with how something is being done. How well you can "roll with it"—and sometimes despite it—will be critical to your career. And life.

People typically change companies several times during the lifespan of a career; those many thousands of media professionals working in the "gig economy" essentially change jobs or companies every time they get a new gig. Those most keenly adept at managing changing circumstances and who can adjust to a variety of people and personalities are the ones that move forward the most—and often more quickly. Those unable or unwilling to adapt are left behind and in the dust. Too many people want to do what you aspire to do to tolerate such inflexibility.

Consistent with ethical values, we must to some degree mold ourselves to fit in, just as others are (hopefully) adjusting to work with you. We also have to learn *when* to be flexible and when to hold our ground. These skills are best gained through the doing, but your willingness to approach work and life with openness and flexibility will yield consequential benefits.

Prepare for the Hardest Interview Questions You'll (Probably) Never Get

Practice your responses to the following "challenging" questions/statements if they were posed during an interview:

Tell me about a time when you were wrong.

What is something you've unlearned?

What's the biggest mistake you ever made and what did you learn from it?

What is the biggest obstacle you've overcome?

When are you least adaptable?

How have you made a situation better?

What is your biggest weakness?

I find that by preparing effective, yet honest, answers for the "hard" questions as well as (of course) for those specifically related to the position/company, you will be more adaptable to, and confident about, whatever questions you are actually asked during the interview. You will have a repertoire of answers to draw from, and you'll likely be "relieved" by the actual questions you get. You'll also gain additional insights about yourself in the process.

Be honest: Are you someone who tends to embrace change, or do you tend to retreat and stick with what you know? In what instances are you more or less adaptable or flexible? This self-understanding and awareness are important in highly collaborative, highly social professions because you will come to know which avenues you are most adept and which you might need help.

Many people are resistant to change. The unknown can be scary. But the unknown can be invigorating and enlivening, an *activator* of your skills and capacities, seeing change as an opportunity to grow and season yourself toward greater successes. As tech consultant Natalie Fratto said, "Adaptability has to be proactive, not reactive. Seek it out, exercise it and flex it like a muscle."[6]

Change is inevitable. It's better to embrace it.

Building Your Adaptability: The Case for Being Well Rounded

Have you ever met someone who, after just a few moments, gives you the strong impression that they could "figure out" almost any task? I know I have. How do we gain this sense of the person? After nearly thirty years as a teacher who helps develop young professionals, I can usually sense this right away, and I soon find out why: They've lived in another country for a period of time; they come from a military family, with constant moves within and outside the United States; they've been a long-term caregiver for a family member. There's an ease with which they approach people and tasks that gives off the vibe that they will figure it out. How valuable this person is to a group or organization when adaptability is so critical!

In almost every conversation I have with successful media leaders and creative people about what it "takes" to be successful for a young or aspiring professional, being "well rounded" is often one of the first things listed. This begs two separate, yet related, questions: What does one really mean by "well rounded"? And why is being well rounded specifically important for enhanced adaptability?

The word "well rounded" is an adjective but is often treated as a noun by the media and entertainment industries. It infers a type of *person* rather than a skill, and a highly desirable person at that. This person is not necessarily viewed as "intelligent" in the strict sense but exhibits curiosity and draws from a range of experiences and knowledge to apply to a variety of situations. Those who are well rounded tend to be convergent thinkers (definition: *a thinker who focuses on the problem as stated and tries to synthesize information and knowledge to achieve a solution*). They are simply better equipped to synthesize various sources of information and then take effective, sometimes even synergistic, action. Well-rounded, adaptable people carry with them figure-it-out qualities that elicit confidence in others through effective action.

Corey, who in the Curiosity attribute challenged himself by taking courses in a variety of areas to supplement his aspirations in audio, used his ongoing curiosity and proactive approach to learn about other departments and technologies within his company. This led him to develop solutions "to problems people didn't know they had, as well as just business practices that not everyone employs that makes me stand out."

"For example, many audio engineers delete their files after handing off to DIT," Corey says. "Not to say this is wrong, it's standard practices. I thought about what would happen if DIT had issues or unforeseen accidents happened, and decided to start as a standard practice to hold files for 1 calendar for free, and if production needed those backups, to offer them at an affordable rate. This has saved a few productions and garnered myself a good rep for doing this."

So how does one become "well rounded"? Certainly, the education system can *help* be an important resource to develop a broad intellectual base to understand history, science, theory, aesthetics, and practical applications from a variety of perspectives. Although developing these "intellectual structures" is important, they are usually not sufficient to characterize a person as well rounded. Additionally, well-rounded people have often "experienced the world," whether through a variety of work experiences (both within and outside the media industries), extended interactions with/in multiple cultures, engagement with ideas beyond their core interests, or a variety of other ways. Moreover, well-rounded people become *seasoned* through experiences with a range of personalities and are better able to navigate with/ through different and perhaps, difficult, personalities. In sum, well-rounded people interact with a variety of intellectual and real-world situations and, thus, are equipped to navigate effectively with new people, new situations, and new (inevitable) problems that require a solution. As such, they draw upon multiple experiences to apply to situations and problems at hand.

It's in *your* power to develop the well roundedness that leads you to be adaptable in critical ways that help you grow and advance over time. In (broadly defined) storytelling industries, it's critical to be able to draw ideas and inspiration from such diverse fields as science, literature, and technology; experience other cultures; and interact with different peoples, races, and religions to build a broad base of perspectives that opens avenues of thought, creativity and possibility. This range of experiences and interactions with the world figuratively, if not literally, opens the mind. An open mind leads to an open-*ness* to adapt, to allow opportunities to come your way, and to develop creative ideas and solutions.

David Epstein, author of *Range*, makes the case for "late specialization" (developing an array of skills before turning focus toward a primary skill), which flies counter to the current culture of U.S. education and training, which emphasizes hyperspecialization, linear thinking, and "tracks" as the best path to develop a talent. Using the very different approach-to-career stories of two legendary athletes, Tiger Woods and Roger Federer, Epstein argues:

> The challenge we all face is how to maintain the benefits of breadth, diverse experience, interdisciplinary thinking, and delayed concentration in a world that increasingly incentivizes, even demands, hyperspecialization. While it is undoubtedly true that there are areas that require individuals with Tiger's precocity and clarity of purpose, as complexity increases—as technology spins the world into vaster webs of interconnected systems in which each individual only sees a small part—we also need more Rogers: people who start broad and embrace diverse experiences and perspectives while they progress. People with range.[7]

If you are *truly* the Tiger Woods of X (whatever it is that you aspire to do in media professions), then go forth. If you are to become the Roger Federer like the vast majority of extraordinary media professionals, you might want to be open to a range of possibilities and how your range of experiences along the way will help forge you into something, into some*one* still uniquely extraordinary. Trust that your well roundedness may well lead to a bigger and better payoff in the longer term. A *lot* of people wind up doing something very different from what they set out to do, and the ones who do this successfully are open and adaptable to these new possibilities; those who are closed off to change and opportunity will likely miss important opportunities. Breadth helps make you more well rounded and adaptable.

ATTRIBUTE TIP FOR CAREER SUCCESS

Embrace the Value of Your Non-Media Work Experiences/Activities

I frequently hear students or early career professionals worry over the "irrelevant" jobs they've had or are doing. Nonsense. Almost every work experience can offer some type of transferability to aid your media-related jobs or internships.

For example, if you've waited tables, you are developing *amazing* skills that will benefit your media jobs: multitasking; serving a variety of customers and an array of coworkers; dealing with and (hopefully) solving problems; how to *be* an energy giver when your energy is not high; and how to stay positive. (You'll also observe how *not* to be.)

It's good to include some non-media work on your resume, especially for internships and early career jobs. They indicate that you have a work ethic, are working your way through school, are able to multitask and do a variety of things, and have a variety of experiences. Don't shy away from including these. Be proud of them and show how they are relevant to the real skills needed for many media positions.

Importantly, *while you're doing them*, proactively *use* those work experiences to enhance your adaptability and, very likely, many of the other attributes found in this book. Your time will feel "less wasted," and you may also find that the job and experience are more rewarding and valuable. Good for everyone!

One exercise I often do with a smaller class is what I call "Blue/Green." I ask students, in thirty seconds, to rapidly scan our immediate surroundings and take mental note of everything they see in the room that is "blue"—*any-thing*—the walls, the floor, what others are wearing, a notebook—*anything* that is blue in their range of sight. I then ask students to close their eyes; I pause for second and then say, "Tell me everything you saw that was *green*." (The look of surprise I see at the change in expectation is worth doing the exercise.) Most have trouble noting anything that was green.

The lesson here—and metaphor, if you will—is that if you're only look-ing for one thing, you're going to miss out on several other possibilities, per-haps equally (if not more) viable or relevant—or at least adding to the variety of what you take in. If we only look for "blue" (a word also associated with depressed feelings), you will inevitably miss out on the green (associated with growth and even money) in life. The more you can see and embrace it all, the more you'll be able to bring to new situations and challenges.

Extraordinary media professionals are not machines. They are emo-tional, passionate, and curious. The best have a dynamic range of interests and interactions with the world through story or travel or work or rela-tionships. Most critically, well-rounded people are equipped to adapt and advance in the content industries. They are intellectually curious, always looking to learn and seek new connections among phenomena and are able to change to fit changed circumstances.

You Are *Not* in Control of Your Career

What is your initial reaction to the heading above?

One of the false beliefs that many of us have—myself included at times—is that we have direct control over our careers and the trajectories of our lives. Very few of us really do. And if it all were known and planned out, would that be entirely satisfying to you? At the very least, it doesn't seem very interesting or particularly helpful in The Big Picture, and key opportu-nities for growth and development will almost certainly be missed.

Your ability to adapt and to go with the flow will be critical. Daniel Mondschain, a production executive at Sony Pictures, describes a career like paddling in a canoe, where you can perhaps control the general direction of where you go but must also navigate currents that can, at times, lead you to drift or even to places you didn't expect.

I'll close with this amazing piece of advice—and life perspective—from Hope Groves, vice president of content technologies at Global Eagle Entertainment, who also lived in London for thirteen years as a media professional:

> Life, your career, your family, etc. are not controlled forces. Sometimes it's great and sometimes it's not. If you continue through the journey with ridged expectations, you'll end up sorely disappointed and blind to the opportunities. If you remain positive and flexible, you'll soon realize that change is good and life is a wonderful gift. Stop trying to predict your future . . . work hard, love fiercely and know that you are enough. It's taken me a long time to figure this out . . . and no matter what your career is, be open to a challenge and change will take you far.

ADAPTABILITY Exercises

1. Describe a specific life experience or situation—perhaps a DM—that has helped or perhaps *forced* you to become more adaptable. In what ways, specifically, did you become more adaptable and how has this impacted you?
2. Read a book or blog, or listen to a podcast, *outside* your core interests. Make lists of new ideas or perspectives you're learning that can benefit your core interests.
3. In which situations do you find yourself to be the most and least adaptable? Make a list of things you are most and least adaptable to.
4. Do something of interest to you that takes you outside your comfort zone. For example, enroll in an improv class or take a class loosely connected to your profession that is much different from what you do (or want to do). How will you have to adapt to this new situation to benefit you going forward?
5. Based on your "dream job" (from Ambition attribute), describe ways in which you will need to be adaptable in order to grow and advance in your career (i.e., how will adaptability enable you to grow/advance in your career?).

Reliability

Being trustworthy or performing consistently well

<u>Synonyms</u>: Dependable, Conscientious, Responsible, Accurate, Stable

<u>Antonyms</u>: Irresponsible, Corrupt, Questionable, Uncertain

Reliability is the quality that leads others not just to believe you but also to believe IN you.

A long day of producing the weekly show for Bompop Radio extended well into the evening. All of the content was "in the can," but a few outstanding technical issues and final editing remained. A lot still to do. Everything had to be resolved for distribution by 8:00 am the next morning. Everyone was stressed, including the boss.

"I'll take care of it," Jaron, an intern, said to his boss. "Everyone can go home."

Sure enough, Jaron stayed up all night, fixing any and all the issues at hand, and the show was ready to air that morning as scheduled.

Jaron's willingness to stay overnight to ensure that the program was ready on time and of high quality was no small gesture and created a mountain of goodwill. But the effect of coming through for his peers and his boss was far greater. Jaron had demonstrated he was someone who could be counted on to come through in a pinch *and* a person who is serious and committed to his profession.

As Jaron ended his internship and was to return to Ohio for his final year of school, his boss found a way to keep paying him. And Jaron had a job waiting for him when he returned to LA after graduation.

"Jaron really saved us that night," his boss told me a few weeks later. "I thought, 'I can't let go of this kid.'"

I asked Jaron what his boss said to him after coming through for him and the group that night. "He said, 'Make yourself so valuable that you're invaluable.'"

Reliability: The Natural Connector

Think of the *things* in your life that you rely on, perhaps your phone or car. Have you ever had your car not start out of the blue or seen a black screen on your phone after you turned it on? How do you feel when that happens? We feel the uncertainties and frustrations acutely when the things we rely on *aren't* reliable (and perhaps take a bit for granted)—or even can't trust "whether" they will work. The lingering doubts impact our day, shape our entire outlook, distract and frustrate us, and drain energy from what we could or should be doing.

Now consider the *people* you can really count on versus those you *can't*. Think of the vast differences in how you feel between the reliable and unreliable people in your life:

* Whom you want to spend more time around (especially on a twelve-hour day)?
* Who can you count on to have your back?
* Who do you consider more honest and trustworthy?
* Who tends to get things done quicker *and better*?
* With whom are you more willing to share information?
* Who is more likely to "own up" to their mistakes and work to correct them?
* Who are you more willing (even eager) to vouch for?
* With whom can you laugh more easily?
* Who are you more inclined to bring onto your team?

All of these answers are easy, of course, but far from unimportant. I hope that you have more reliable than unreliable people in your life, but you likely haven't dislodged all of the unreliable people because you cannot control everyone who populates your peer group, your work environments, or perhaps even your family. This only increases the value of those core people you can *really* count on.

We can take our daily functions for granted, like a phone or car, until we don't have them anymore. But when *people* in our daily lives can't be trusted, miss deadlines, don't pull their own weight, and make costly and unnecessary mistakes, the consequences of unreliability are much greater in The Big Picture of your life and career. It can spread like a deadly wildfire that snuffs out opportunity and possibility for you and your relationship network.

Confucius put it even more bluntly: "A man who is unreliable is utterly useless."

I am often asked to recommend someone I know—a student or alum—for an entry-level job or internship. Those who have shown themselves to be unreliable, regardless of talent or grades, will *never* be recommended. Media professionals will tell you the same thing. Why? We simply aren't willing to put our own reputations on the line for someone who is known by us to be unreliable. But those who have shown themselves to be consistently reliable will surely benefit from the praises we are apt to sing.

In the previous chapter, I noted that adaptability was assessed by media professionals as the most important attribute toward career success. Reliability was second most important.[1] Both of these attributes are "connected" to Connective in the 12 Attributes Model because those who consistently demonstrate adaptability and reliability *organically* connect with their relationship network. Your strong bonds with other adaptable, reliable professionals will endure through the changes and uncertainties that abound within the media industries. You will be highly valued within an organization or group *and* highly referenced to others inside and outside your network. Your peers and colleagues will say good things about you—vouch for you!—when you don't even know it. What a powerful idea!

Reliability is the one attribute you *must* develop NOW—made into an enduring habit—if you plan to succeed in the media professions. We simply want to work with people—be *around* people—we can rely on to do good work, who roll with the punches, and who consistently come through in a pinch. Successful media professionals feel liberated to be creative and resourceful when they are surrounded with reliable people.

Reliability begets trust; trust begets opportunity. Be worthy of Trust. Be trustworthy.

ATTRIBUTE TIP FOR CAREER SUCCESS

It's Better to Eat Crow When It's Warm
(aka Own Up to Your Mistakes, Then Don't Repeat Them)

One of my dad's favorite sayings was "It's better to eat crow when it's warm than when it's cold." This means that when you make a mistake, it's better to own up to the mistake sooner rather than later. Crow (the bird) is going to taste bad either way, but it's not nearly as bad when it's fresh and identified rather than not acknowledged and allowed to fester into something worse.

You *will* make mistakes in your career and on the job. But most of them will be forgiven if you own up to them, learn from them, don't make the same mistakes again, and show growth as a result. Some of your mistakes might be from trying too hard, some might be because you didn't know the right/best questions to ask, and some might be because you didn't pay careful enough attention.

So when you *have* to eat crow, make sure you eat it warm.

In the media industries—the "Business of People," to coin a phrase I heard from TV producer Randall Winston—collaboration is central. Time is money and a precious commodity. Deadlines loom and uncertainties abound. Your personal reliability will be a big key to your success. Why do many of the great film directors, TV producers, and musicians tend to have the same core collaborators from project to project? These collaborators (e.g., mixing engineers, DPs, editors) are obviously extremely competent but additionally valued because their reliability and familiarity create a "short hand" to increase efficiency (save time). Professionals that can deliver dependably at a consistently high level are a proverbial comfort blanket and will be more valued.

It's time to be very honest with yourself. If you aren't as reliable as you could be—*must* be—NOW is the time to develop strategies to improve this critical attribute. Identify what things are getting in your way and preventing you from being as reliable as you can be. People do notice unreliability—showing up late, not turning things in on deadline, or not doing something correctly due to inattention—and this will hold you back even if you don't directly see it. You have a response-*ability* to take action to be more reliable and accountable.

If you can honestly assess that you are highly reliable and can be consistently be counted on—especially when it's not convenient or particularly inspiring to you—recognize that the most critical, highly-bonded relationships in your life and career are founded in the trust that you are fostering for yourself and hold in high value for others. Keep going. Build upon this habit because it will be highly valued throughout your career.

Reliability Is Built on the Little Things You Can Control (So Do Them Well)

"Besides all the technical, geeky, aspects that come to music production, I've been genuinely surprised from the amount of clients that have complimented my ability to simply label things correctly, properly fill out paperwork, and respond properly to e-mails," says Jaron Takach, who made himself "invaluable" at the beginning of this attribute and is now a rising musician/producer/engineer. "It's true that the little things go a long way in retaining clients."

In the competitive, collaborative media professions, be aware that you are constantly being *assessed*. Not in some judge-y way, but professionals are nevertheless consciously and subconsciously thinking about who they do and don't want to work with, who they might bring to the next project or opportunity, who is making their time better or worse, who they might be more or less willing to help and mentor. If you're aspiring or early in your career, be aware of this. As you get a foothold in the industry, you'll be assessing, too.

Let's take a look at some of these "little things" that working, successful media professionals notice.

Arrive Early, Stay Late

A common adage in the media professions is "If you're on time, you're late; if you're late, you're fired." This speaks to the value (and cost) of time lost in production or in the office. But more directly, it speaks to the competitive nature of the media and entertainment professions. There are many people who would love to have the job you have (however minor and low on the totem pole), and lateness will lead to you not getting called back or to outright firing. People want to see that you are dependable, and they want to see your commitment day in and day out.

Those who arrive early every day are noticed for all the right reasons; those who barely make it on time or arrive a few minutes late are noticed for negative reasons. If you have a reputation as someone who is there before almost everyone else, it sends a big, positive message that you're ready and committed to work, even (perhaps especially) if your work is currently mundane and uninspiring. This won't likely be expressed to you if you consistently arrive early ("Wow, thanks for being early every day!"), but do not be fooled into thinking that when you arrive isn't being noticed. And, as a slight bonus, on those scant days when an unavoidable issue occurs—e.g., a car accident (hopefully not involving you), a doctor's appointment—you will be cut some slack because you've put in enough early arrival deposits to justify being late.

KEY WAYS TO ENSURE YOUR RELIABILITY

Do what you say you're going to do
Arrive early and (be willing to) stay late
Meet deadlines
Don't overcommit
Under promise and over deliver
Finish what you start
Pay attention to details
Don't make the same mistake twice
Do things right the first time
Listen carefully and genuinely
Be prepared
Ask the right questions
Treat *everyone* with kindness and respect

Your willingness—even habit—to stay after the work day ends can have valuable rewards. This doesn't suggest staying up all night like Jaron did, but the little offers of committing extra time. Staying an extra fifteen minutes to help your boss, peer, or colleague to finish a task that might be no more than a few minutes of your time can have monumental impact on your coworkers and, *especially*, your relationships with them. Always remember: The most valuable commodity to successful professionals is their *time*. If you can make someone else's time better, shorter, and/or easier, you will generate valuable "points" for yourself that far exceeds the actual time spent.

Write It Down

Early in his career, Daniel Mondschain, now a production executive at Sony Pictures, worked as an assistant for a producer who gave him a list of verbal instructions on tasks she needed to have completed. Daniel responded, "I got it."

"Why aren't you writing this down?" she asked.

"I got it," Daniel replied.

"I want you to write it down, because I don't want to spend time *wondering* whether you're going to do correctly what I've asked."

The most common complaint I hear about interns and early career professionals involves not paying careful attention to details. Not doing things right the first time seeds doubt that will negatively affect your short- and long-term opportunities (and advancement). Your job, especially early on, often involves tasks that more experienced and advanced colleagues don't want to spend time on. When you help create efficiencies for others you're actually helping yourself because you're adding value to your role, becoming indispensable in the process. I refer to this as "leverage," because your high-quality work and ability to pay attention to details adds power to what you offer.

So, carry a notepad with you whenever you're at work. A notepad carries both practical and symbolic power. In a practical sense, if you write down what is needed when asked by a boss or colleague, you're much more likely to do it correctly the first time. In communication, accuracy gets lost when just hearing something. (Have you ever gotten instructions or come to agreement on what to do, but in the time lapse forget exactly what you needed to do?) The notepad can also be useful to you because you can also jot down your own ideas and thoughts throughout the day. *Symbolically*, you're demonstrating to others that you are prepared and have a desire to get details right the first time.

During the first week of our LA program, just before students begin their internships, I hand out six-by-nine-inch yellow notepads to each student and explain why "writing it down" is of critical practical and symbolic importance. Without fail, students will tell me the next week that a supervisor favorably made note that they were ready to write down what needed to be done, sending the message that the intern wanted to get it right. This immediately started the relationship on a positive note and these students almost always had rewarding experiences and were eventually (sooner than later relative to most) given more interesting things to do.

Prep, Prep, Prep

Vance Van Petten, president of the Producers Guild of America, will ask aspiring professionals during a negotiation seminar what is the most important thing in a negotiation. Vance receives a lot of good answers, but almost never the most important one: Preparation! Taking steps to be as prepared as possible, to think of every angle, to anticipate questions and answers, to think through possibilities *before* the task, meeting, or interaction will put you in better position to produce more effective results. You're taking initiative in the service of your own reliability and the payoff over time will be well worth it.

Be True to Yourself and the Results Will Be, Too

One myth of the creative and media industries—a dangerous one I believe—is that you have to become something you're not in order to succeed. Absolute nonsense! In fact, the opposite is true. You want to be as authentically *you* as possible at all times.

But be your best you! This will make your unique qualities shine through *and* people will know you for who *you* are and that will serve as the foundation for a strong, trusting, *better* relationship. You'll be more likely to know who *they* are, too—both positive and negative—if you're being your most authentic self. Don't worry about being perfect—like 100 percent of the rest of us—but be aware of any key imperfections you might have so that you continue to strive to be better *and* continually seek to surround yourself with people who help mitigate your gaps. If you are true to your best, authentic self, you'll consistently meet expectations—and often exceed them over time.

Just as the arrows in the 12 Attributes Model show us, this all goes back to YOU and remaining true to the important values that guide your decisions and aspirations. Know that your personal growth and desire to continually learn are lifelong pursuits. At any point—at *every* point if at all possible—your actions and decisions should be in alignment with your core values. This can only be determined by you and enacted by you. Recognize that some of your values *will* shift to some degree as you reach various stages of your life and career. Don't compromise your values, but remain flexible and open to new ideas and opportunities found by highly adaptable, inquisitive media professionals.

If you are reliable and place high value on being a reliable person, the resulting impacts on your life and career will reflect that over time. Similarly, if you lack reliability and do not value it, your results will be true to that, too.

Consider how being "true" impacts various aspects of life and work:

* In science, reliability is highly valued because it indicates the internal consistency and stability of a measuring device.
* In golf, the greatest players have what is called a "repeatable swing," meaning they can consistently repeat the same swing and motion time after time, which creates consistently great results.
* In baseball, pitchers with a "repeatable delivery" more consistently put the ball where they want it, using an assortment of pitches for great effectiveness.
* Directors, producers, and performers who reliably attract audiences, users, or buyers (hence revenue) to their medium or platform are more likely to be given financing and earn more money for future work.
* Those who succeed in live television or in broadcast/electronic journalism are on time and meet deadlines consistently. They are like a clock.

Be your own clock. If you are true to yourself and strive to enact the attributes found in this book—Reliability being a key one—people will come to know you for who you *are* and the results will take care of themselves.

The media and creative industries do not suffer fools kindly or for very long. There are others seeking to do what you aspire to do, however mundane or uninspiring it might seem in the moment. The popular press tells of egotistical stars who only think of themselves and create havoc for everyone. These people represent a small fraction of the workforce in the creative industries. The large majority's very paychecks depend on how dependable they are, how they come through in a pinch, and how reliable they are to get things done *each and every time*.

I want to end our discussion on Reliability by sharing my dad's all-time favorite story. He called it "The Dog Story." Here's how it goes:

A man happened upon a roadside shop, often called in the South a what-not shop because it sold a variety of knick-knacks that you can see from the road. But this particular what-not shop only had carved wooden dogs lining the road outside the store. The carved dogs were of all shapes and sizes. The man marveled at how beautiful and life-like the wooden dogs were.

The man went inside the store, where he found shelves and shelves of nothing but carved wooden dogs of all shapes and sizes. He found the shopkeeper.

"These dogs are *so* amazing and life-like," the man said. "How do you make them all look so realistic?"

"There's nothing to it," the shopkeeper replied. "You take a block of wood and anything that doesn't look like a dog, you cut it away."

For me, "The Dog Story" says that no matter what you're presented with, big or small, if you focus on what you have, know what you want to use it toward, and make the best of it, you'll have consistent results and will amaze people through your dedication to even the most mundane things.

By cutting away what's not needed to accomplish your goals, you get to the core of what really matters to you.

Only *you* can make your Dog a reality.

RELIABILITY Exercises

1. Make a list of people in your life who you can completely rely upon or trust (who will come through for you when you need them). Describe a list of specific actions or activities—however big or small—for each person you list that demonstrate this high level of reliability and trust to you.

2. Describe at least one situation in which you willingly remained (stayed overtime) to help someone complete a task (finish work needed) or resolve a problem (e.g., help someone repair a flat tire). This could be at work, an organization, or a personal assist. What response did you get for going "above and beyond"? Did this lead to tangible or intangible benefits in the short or long term?

3. Describe a person in your life who is NOT reliable. Describe in specific detail the actions and experiences that lead you to this conclusion.

4. What areas of your life are you least reliable (e.g., arriving late, not paying attention to details, lack of preparation, procrastination, not being good to your word, missing deadlines, or making correctable mistakes) and most need to work on? What strategies will you develop to improve these "weaknesses" in your reliability? Use goal setting to improve your reliability.

Integrity

Firm adherence to a code of especially moral or artistic values

Synonyms: Character, Virtue, Decency, Reputation, Honesty, Sincerity
Antonyms: Dishonest, Corrupt, Immoral, Deceitful, Dishonorable, Ill Repute

> Real integrity is doing the right thing, knowing that nobody's going
> to know whether you did it or not.
> —Oprah Winfrey

Success without Integrity Is Failure

Every attribute offered in this book is important to your career and success. But I believe you *can* be extraordinary without being extraordinary at each and every attribute.

Integrity is different.

You cannot be extraordinary without personal integrity.

A person can acquire financial wealth and powerful titles, lavish house(s), and the most expensive car(s) and even do great, high-quality work admired by millions. But if this is achieved outside the foundations of integrity, it means little to nothing in The Big Picture of life and career. No amount of money made, millions who've been influenced, or number of awards received can compensate for the lack of integrity.

And the consequences to that person can be quite extraordinary (and public), even as the person is quite obviously not.

The "Me Too Movement" brought into focus how some powerful, accomplished players in the media and entertainment industries used their power to take advantage of people, particularly women, in disgusting, repugnant ways. The Harvey Weinsteins and Roger Ailes of our world were—emphasis on the word *were*—brilliant, successful, and accomplished, except where it really mattered. Where it *only* mattered. In fact, how they treated people, what they were willing to do to get their way, and the manner in which they held power over others wash away the material successes and any respect they once enjoyed, and diminish to some degree the names and associations to them.

As a current or aspiring media professional, you are by definition involved in creating content for *public* consumption—sometimes for hundreds, sometimes for millions. If your name is associated with it, it's around forever. That's part of the allure of what you want to do. You want your work and involvement in it to be seen in the best positive light, heightened by your own contributions and to those with whom you associate.

Integrity is not always easy to come by in the media professions. In fact, it can be quite difficult at times. There are daily financial pressures and deadlines. It's competitive with ego-driven strivers seeking to move up in their world. People can easily get carried away with the perceived importance of their own work and/or personal value.

There is a minority of people that can get away with this—for a while. These are usually people who have shown themselves able to generate money for others and are sometimes "allowed" to get away with bad behavior that's "looked away from" to maintain the gravy train of revenue and profits. These people do exist in the media and entertainment industries. And you will undoubtedly, at times, interact with these people. But integrity and success are *not* mutually exclusive concepts.

Getting to the Root of Your Integrity

The root word for integrity is "integer," which means whole, pure, entire, and undiminished.[1] This is a very useful way to think of your own integrity, because integrity isn't a part-time pursuit. Integrity isn't built from expediency or doing what is most convenient or easy in the moment or (especially) when it comes at the expense of others. When you have integrity, you are whole and you cannot be diminished by challenges to your own integrity or by circumstances that might be outside your control. In fact, your integrity is strengthened—made *more* whole—by the tests and challenges to it. At the end of the day—each day or at the end of your life—you want to look in the mirror and be satisfied that your personal integrity remained intact.

CHARACTER TRAITS RELATED TO INTEGRITY[2]

Gracious—express gratitude and recognize achievements for people they work with

Honest—strive to be truthful, own up to mistakes, and learn from them

Trustworthy—follow through with commitments

Hardworking—produce high-quality work on time, regardless of task

Responsible—take accountability for actions; they are organized and proactive to deliver

Helpful—help those in need, lending time for a project, or offer to cover in an emergency

Patient—tolerate challenges, delays, and unexpected obstacles with a calm, even demeanor

Integrity is the moral compass you carry with you that governs the decisions you make in life, career, and business; the ways you treat others; how you respond to difficulties and challenges; and, ultimately, why others with integrity will want to continue a working relationship with you, thus only fortifying your own integrity.

It's critical to connect yourself with those people. To *be* one of those people.

A misperception about the media professions is that it's totally cut-throat and you have to be like that in order to succeed. However, in my own personal experience and observation, there are many extraordinary people who succeed wildly and also exhibit great integrity. They are generous, supportive, and willing to mentor. They are also driven and passionate strivers with focus and limited time. Many of the best will devote themselves to young or aspiring professionals who they see in themselves. In many cases, someone else took a "flyer" *on them* somewhere along the way or, if not, they feel a desire to give of themselves in ways they didn't receive. They *feel* fortunate to do what they do and willingly pay it forward.

Be that person, too. You'll do the same for others in due time.

The media industries also have a reputation for being particularly tough on younger professionals; those trying to make their way into and up these highly competitive industries, who believe they must "put up with" almost anything as part of the "initiation" into these highly desirable careers. If you're a young professional, you don't have to endure such terrible treatment, and no one has the right to treat you that way. And know that you cannot be truly extraordinary if you treat people similarly or believe this is the pathway to the top.

This doesn't imply that your career should be made "easier" or that you won't/shouldn't deal with struggle as your career takes shape. You will in all likelihood begin in roles beneath your education level and talents. You may take on tasks that are uninspiring to you. You may have bosses that don't have your best interests at heart. But your personal integrity should never waver, and the foundations of your core values should remain and, in fact, become stronger as you interact with the positive and, sometimes, negative forces in your work world. This is all part of the process of learning and growing toward figuring out what you truly are most motivated to do. Your willingness to work hard without entitlement should be part of the core values founded in integrity. These experiences should only serve to build, strengthen, and reinforce your character rather than diminish it.

ATTRIBUTE TIP FOR CAREER SUCCESS

Don't Burn Bridges—EVER

You will likely, at some point in your work life, be fired or let go. This may or may not be due to things in your control. Or, perhaps you'll work with someone you can't stand and move on to another job (hopefully sooner than later). Take responsibility for, and learn from, the experiences. But don't burn the bridge. EVER.

If you burn a bridge with someone—no matter how justified you might feel, no matter how at fault the other person might be, and no matter how good it might feel in the moment (and it can sometimes feel good in the moment)—be aware that the person will have occasion to talk about you if your name comes up (or may talk negatively about you voluntarily). Words and actions travel, both negatively and positively. They can travel like wildfire, bringing either the positive heat of opportunities and access or the charred remains of a once-promising career burned to the ground. Just like burning down an actual bridge, it may take years to repair or reconstruct your reputation, even if unwarranted. So minimize any damage within your control.

However, when what you do—or what you are asked to do and *be*—runs counter to your moral and ethical values (look at the antonyms at the beginning of this chapter), you have the right—the *self-duty*—to maintain your integrity and say no. Have confidence that it will work out over time, leading you to make even better distinctions about yourself, your career, and the *right* people in your life and career. The people that really matter in your life will respect you for it, those who don't won't, and trust that this will all lead to good things in the all-important Big Picture.

Contrast this with the opposite. Do you really want to live life taking advantage of others? Getting by, getting through, without earning it? Through dishonesty and exploitation? Have you known or worked with people like this? Wonder how they can live with themselves? People with integrity exhibit consistent behaviors and don't look for the easy ways out. They treat *everyone* with respect. Those who lack integrity are not whole. In fact, there's a gaping *hole* in the attributes suitcase that will be discovered sooner or later, spilling out and undermining other good attributes they may have to offer.

When you get to the end of your career, whatever career that is, how do you want to see yourself? How do you want others to view you? What legacy do you want to leave behind? The most solid foundation is built on the bedrock of your personal integrity and core values that guide the decisions you make and ways you treat people in your relationship network.

Integrity is aligned next to Reliability in the 12 Attributes Model because there are obvious ties between them. People who are trustworthy and dependable tend to offer integrity. They are more principled and accountable through their actions. Likewise, those with integrity are responsible and consistent in their actions and behaviors toward themselves and others. They build deep mutual bonds in their relationship network because of these virtues. Integrity is built on the shoulders of working hard, working smart, treating others well, involving yourself with content and people that you take pride in, and helping others along the way. Trust that money will follow in due time, will seem almost *incidental*, when grounded in the integrity you consistently demonstrate over time.

Your Reputation Is *Everything* . . . and It Precedes You

Answer the following questions as truthfully as possible:

Do you work hard—and smart?
Are you fun to be around, even when things aren't going great?
Do you always arrive on time, usually early?
Do you stand up for what is right?
Can you roll with the (figurative) punches?
Do you do what you say you're going to do?
Do you treat *everyone* with kindness, tact, and respect at all times?

The answers to these questions (and others) form the basis upon which people assess your reputation. In the social, shockingly small world that is the media professions, your reputation is almost always built from other's opinions about you rather than your own. People talk. Words travel. People rely on recommendations from people who've already had experiences with you—usually before they meet you. (Your LinkedIn and various social media sites will be checked, too.) The better *their* reputation, the more the value placed on their opinion of *you*. Your hard skills, while important, almost always takes a secondary role to your personal behavior in the assessment process.

And reputation works both ways. You may get some opportunities—some of which you never knew about or applied for—through people who know you and can vouch enthusiastically for you. You may get passed over for opportunities—which you may or may not know existed—when people speak less than enthusiastically about you. The *perception* of a bad reputation is just about as damaging as *having* a bad reputation.

"I've seen too many people when they get a bad reputation then have difficulty getting work," says veteran production executive Kevin Hamburger. "The stakes are so high in this business that sometimes people don't get a second chance . . . even if they should."

You will talk, too, often staking your own reputation on the words you speak about those you know and work with (or worked with). You will be most positive about those you know will prove you right, and most reluctant to endorse those that might prove you wrong. Your word will gain additional resonance with others as you gain experience and advance, expand and deepen your relationship network, and grow into positions of greater influence. You'll place even more emphasis on the value of reputation in the development and maintenance of your career.

ATTRIBUTE TIP FOR CAREER SUCCESS

Focus on Your Strengths First

"I find that when someone wants to build a reputation, that the best way to start is to reflect on the work you have just done to pinpoint what you enjoy and/or where you feel you're successful," says Hope Groves, a twenty-year veteran in the industry. "Working on your reputation [by] focusing on your weaknesses is a battle that probably isn't worth winning. Usually people's weaknesses are reflective of something they don't like and who wants to be known for something they don't like? So, like when you are building your brand, be self-reflective on what you want be known for and build a plan of action around that reputation."

I once asked development executive Richard Gold how reputation influences his decisions about people:

I certainly go on other people I trust's word-of-mouth and point-of-view. If I don't already have a sense of their reputation, I'll certainly ask a colleague or a close friend. Otherwise, word travels very quickly in our industry, so I usually will hear things through the grapevine about people who I should be wary of. I like to give people the benefit of the doubt always, but I also have been around long enough at this point to know that when there's smoke, there's often fire. And if all else fails, I just go on instinct—I'm a big believer in listening to your gut, and I don't think you can survive for very long in this business without really strong instincts. So I just listen to my "spidey sense," and if I ever feel some sort of hesitation, even if there's not a rational explanation behind it, I always pause to consider and listen to that part of myself.

Notice how thoughts and questions about reputation seem connected to one's reliability. They are, but there's more to it. In the field of science, reliability is a highly valued term because it indicates the relative internal consistency of a measure (i.e., you can demonstrate similar results time after time). But there's a related term of equal importance in science. *Validity* reveals the relative "truth" of a measure. You can reliably get consistent results, but if the results do not accurately explain the concept, reliability has no real value.

Thus, you "can" be reliable without having integrity, but your reliability has little real value over time if it's not founded in integrity. You are what people think you are—even if you aren't—so make sure this represents the best you have to offer. Reliability without validity (i.e., integrity) can lead you to the same results but down the wrong paths or, as journalist Ernesto Herrera once stated, "Competence without integrity is meaningless, even dangerous."

True integrity is reliably doing what's right all the time.

REALLY OLD QUOTES THAT STILL HOLD TRUE

It takes many good deeds to build a good reputation, and only one bad one to lose it.—Benjamin Franklin

Reputation, reputation, reputation! O, I have lost my reputation, I have lost the immortal part of myself, and what remains is bestial!—William Shakespeare

The way to gain a good reputation is to endeavor to be what you desire to appear.—Socrates

A single lie destroys a whole reputation of integrity.—Baltasar Gracian

A good reputation is more valuable than money.—Publilius Syrus

Character is like a tree and reputation like a shadow. The shadow is what we think of it; the tree is the real thing.—Abraham Lincoln

You can't build a reputation on what you're going to do.—Henry Ford

Ninety percent of the politicians give the other ten percent a bad reputation.—Henry Kissinger

If you answered "yes" to most or all of the questions at the top of this section, you are well on your way to having a reliable *and* valid reputation with results both consistent and true over time. You will demonstrate these great attributes externally to the benefit of your career and live with them internally so that you're on the right track, even if the tracks may change over time.

Remember from the Connective chapter that "it's who you know and who knows you *for the right reasons*." If your reputation is bad, or even if people *perceive* that you have a bad reputation, this will negatively impact your opportunities to get work and advance, especially in the longer term. Bad reputations can come from a poor work ethic or repeatedly showing up late (or sometimes not at all). If people can't trust you, they won't put their own reputation on the line on your behalf. You want people to remember you for all the right reasons—reasons that will have people asking you back, giving you that extra time or opportunity that those with lesser reputations do not enjoy. You want others to readily, effortlessly, place you "top of mind" for all the right reasons so that people vouch for you with enthusiasm. This happens best when it's by-product of not only what you *do* but also who you *are*.

But, even in an alternate reality where a bad reputation didn't eventually catch up to you, is this really how you want to live your life? Is this the person you want to see in the mirror as you wake up each day and go to bed each night? One of my favorite songs is "Minutes to Memories" by John Mellencamp, which contains perhaps my favorite line from any song: "An honest man's pillow is his peace of mind." Living with honesty and integrity really does matter as you forge a life and career in these crazy, unpredictable, at times unfair, professions. As you build relationships that deepen, as you perhaps have family and influence the next generations of media professionals, your personal integrity remains your bedrock, your foundation, to do great things consistently *the right way*. Without that, you cannot be truly extraordinary.

Integrity and You(r) Attributes

Developing and using the attributes described in this book should lead you to value the importance of integrity as you build and sustain a career in the media and creative professions. Why? Because it all starts with YOU. Who you are determines what you experience daily and in The Big Picture. It sounds cliché, but you must live with yourself twenty-four hours a day and that person should be someone you are comfortable with, making decisions in alignment with on your own personal values. Your integrity is what allows you to sleep at night and treat people with respect and dignity.

The 12 Attributes Model is premised on the high achievement of many, if not all, of the attributes. In combination, they enhance your reputation as a result of your passion, ambition, connections, your persistence and resiliency, your curiosity, your willingness to adapt, and your reliability over time. The development of these attributes will serve to reinforce *you* to believe in yourself and your ability to bounce back from any setback.

Ultimately, *who you are* is more important than the "things" you acquire. But who you are is manifest to some degree through your career-related accomplishments. These can be traditional career measures (e.g., money, title), but they should also be how you raised and attended to your children; how you helped others in need; how you "paid it forward" to help other young, aspiring professionals get on a path to success, and the many other ways you can contribute.

In the end—and when it's near the end—media professionals with integrity don't measure themselves by how much money they've made or the titles they held. They are instead focused on the relationships and experiences that brought meaning to their lives and to the lives of others. The things that once perhaps seemed so important aren't so relevant anymore.

The 7 Habits of Highly Effective People offers a brilliant visualization exercise where you are observing your own funeral. When your time on earth is all said and done, what would you want a friend, a coworker, and a family member to say about you?

This might seem a bit morbid to you at first, but try it. Really visualize, *emotionalize* what you would want these people to say about you. Then strive to be that person in your life going forward.

INTEGRITY Exercises

1. Think of a specific person you consider to be of high integrity. Make a list of qualities that you see in that person. What specific observations have you made about the person's behavior that demonstrates integrity? What can you learn from this example to apply to your own life?
2. Describe a person in your life that you *dis*trust. Describe in detail the actions and experiences that lead you to this conclusion? What have you learned *not* to do?
3. Describe an instance where you had to stand up for what is right, even when it came at personal cost (or went against the majority in your group). How did this make you feel? Why were you compelled to stand up in this instance?
4. Identify a specific person you consider to have (1) a good reputation and (2) a bad reputation. What specific interactions lead you to assess each person that way? Did you know of the respective reputations prior to meeting each person?
5. Look at the "hierarchy of values" you created for the YOU attribute (or do this exercise again here after you've reflexively interacted with the first ten attributes). What do they say about you and your priorities? In what ways could you use this understanding to be accountable for yourself (or more so) and your career aspirations?

Part IV

The Reinforcing Attributes

To make stronger or more effective

People's beliefs about their abilities have a profound effect on those abilities. Beliefs are determinants of how people think, behave, and feel; how we perceive situations and how we behave in response to different situations. Beliefs in personal efficacy affect life choices, level of motivation, quality of function, resilience to adversity and vulnerability to stress and depression.
—Albert Bandura

Bandura's pioneering concept of self-efficacy plays a monumental role in our personal and professional lives and serves as a key *self-reinforcing* function for successful media professionals. When people learn how to bounce back from challenges/problems or develop confidence based on positive outcomes, motivation is boosted, increasing one's belief in their abilities.[1]

Your self-efficacy becomes a self-fulfilling prophecy, reinforcing your confidence and resilience as you navigate these difficult, sometimes unfair, yet enticing careers. You believe in the likelihood of accomplishing a task and can handle the emotional outcome of anything. You face opportunities and challenges of life realistically, but with optimism. You deal with them effectively, practicing "positive self-talk" to build strength and confidence in the process. Combined with—perhaps *driven* by—the various attributes offered before them, the Reinforcing Attributes give you both the self-assuredness and the wherewithal to achieve more while remaining consistent with your passions and deeper values. Like building muscle, they strengthen your capacities to do more, to want more, and to *be* more.

Confidence

Earned self-assurance in one's powers, abilities, or capacities

Synonyms: Faith, Self-Esteem, Certainty, Courage, Poise

Antonyms: Self-Doubt, Fear, Hesitation, Arrogance, Insecurity

(W)ith confidence and by believing in yourself, you can accomplish any goal.

—Queen Latifah

In the 2019 Netflix documentary *Dolly Parton: Here I Am*, we see ground breaking journalist Barbara Walters ask the legendary country singer about her persona in a 1977 interview:

Walters: You don't have to look like this. You're very beautiful. You don't have to wear the blond wigs, you don't have to wear the extreme clothes, right?

Dolly: It's certainly a choice. I don't like to be like everybody else. I've often made the statement that I would never stoop so low to be fashionable. That's the easiest thing in the world to do. So I just decided I would do something that at least would get the attention. Once they got past the shock of the ridiculous way I looked, then they would see there was parts of me to be appreciated. Show business is a money-making joke and I always liked telling jokes.

Walters: But do you ever feel that you're a joke, that people make fun of you?

Dolly: Oh, I know they make fun of me. But actually all these years the people has thought the joke was on me, but it's actually been on the public. I know exactly what I'm doing, and I can change it at any time.

If you *knew* you could succeed at something—anything—that's important or meaningful to you, what is that "something" you would choose to do? What steps you would be willing to take to get there? Who would you be willing to engage with? What levels of effort would you exert toward that meaningful goal if you *knew* you'd accomplish it? Would you be more inclined to take risks if you knew it would work out in the end?

What if you had *freedom from doubt*?

This is one of the definitions for confidence, something Dolly Parton certainly exhibits, and a useful way to think about the influence confidence can play in our pursuits of the things we desire in life and career. Many of us live in doubt, wondering if we're doing (and saying) the right things, moving in the right directions, making the right choices in our lives and careers. We doubt ourselves and our abilities. We look around us, perhaps at peers with similar age/experience range who are succeeding beyond where we currently are, and that only reinforces our self-doubts.

But look at some of the key words in the exchange between Barbara Walters and Dolly Parton. Choice. Decide. Change. Fun. Those with confidence in themselves, like Dolly Parton and other extraordinary media and creative professionals, find a way to free themselves to make decisions for themselves that make sense *to them*, to think and act for themselves, and to not live in fear of "doing it wrong." They feel empowered to say "no" to things that don't feel right, and keep moving forward when they hear "no." They make active choices about their direction but know they can adapt at any time.

ATTRIBUTE TIP FOR CAREER SUCCESS

Focus on *Your* Success—*Not* on the Successes of Others

In the nonlinear, sometimes unfair, media professions, you may at times witness people you know with less experience and/or talent get an opportunity or promotion. This can be difficult for you, provoking envy and self-doubt as you feel like people are passing "over" you.

However, a common piece of advice I hear from media professionals, particularly for younger professionals, is to *not* focus on successes and opportunities that others are gaining. This is admittedly easier said than done. In fact, it can be incredible difficult and deflating at times—if you let it. But if you focus on your envy and allow yourself to get down about what you're not attaining, you're only draining time and energy away from what you could be, *should be* doing in the service of our own goals and skills development. Ultimately, focus on what you can do rather than the envy you might feel. Be happy for the person, see what you can learn about why the person got the opportunity, use this as positive fuel toward your own goals, and keep working on you.

Earned confidence serves to help lift the weight of self-doubt that often stops us from pursuing the "dreams" and "goals" we seek—those things that enrich our personal and professional lives. Even when we can't yet predict or connect every dot along our pathways, we can keep moving toward those things we're drawn to confident in knowing that good things will happen. Freedom from doubt liberates us to do more and to *be* more.

"Confidence is a direct path to freedom in your career," says Micah Upshaw, an early career TV journalist. "When you believe in yourself, other people will believe in you, too. It allows you to make decisions that are best for you and it allows you to say yes or no to opportunities rather than someone making a decision for you."

The key (and obvious) question is: How do we free ourselves from doubt?

Confidence Is an Acquired Skill

Even as you might feel naturally inclined to be more confident about certain skills or aptitudes than others, earned confidence is an *acquired* skill. It's developed. It's incremental. It's honed in the doing, through effective practice with technical (hard) skills needed for specific tasks related to your interests *and* with broader (soft) skills needed to work with people to get things done. As you gain more hard and soft skills specific to your profession, you'll tend to gain more confidence in your capacities to do and handle more—even the new things you've yet to encounter. Just as you can't gain sustainable strength through one session of weight training, you can't expect to have confidence overnight.

"I believe confidence is essential when approaching any decision or opportunity," says Earl Hopkins, an early career journalist. "Without confidence it's easy to get sidetracked by other's opinions. Often, we undervalue ourselves due to a lack of confidence. It's important we truly define what skills we possess, what we offer and how beneficial the decision we make will be for us at the end."

Tre Wright, a rising music producer/artist, agrees. "Confidence plays a huge factor, especially in the music industry. A lot of times lack of confidence leads to over-thinking creative decisions, as well as 'playing it safe,' and not trying to push your craft forward or to be innovative. Also, people can tell when you lack confidence and might not come to you for the bigger opportunities if they sense that."

"Your career growth is dependent on your value," says entertainment entrepreneur Dylan Berry. "Your value is based on your convictions and your capability of executing those convictions. Confidence is the vehicle that allows you to win over a room and have them accept that you are the person to execute your convictions however crazy or out of the box they may be."

Let's be clear that earned self-confidence is not the same as its ugly cousin: arrogance. Don't mistake arrogance (or its even uglier cousin, narcissism) for confidence. "Yes, you will meet plenty of arrogant and successful entertainment industry professionals—and might even be fooled to think this arrogance is a strength," Berry says. "But trust me, it is not productive if you want a sustainable career and often ends in a lonely dismal fall from grace resulting in no career at all. Those that last in the business act honorably and have respect for what they don't know, but still have the confidence to passionately fight for what they believe is the right chess move to make."

"Arrogance is a sure sign of a confidence problem," Berry adds. "It's an over correction to lack of confidence in my mind or it is simply delusional. Either way, arrogance holds little value to productivity in a creative pursuit.

"In short, the right kind of confidence is good, the wrong kind is useless and sucking the air out of the room."

You needn't be confident with everything you do, but you need to develop confidence over time that you can *figure out* almost anything pertinent to getting things done effectively. Somewhat counterintuitively, the most confident people are the ones often *asking* the questions—the right questions—rather than appearing to have all of the answers.

"It seems like you don't master confidence as much as you get better at learning how to ask the right questions at the right time to help with decision making," says writer and showrunner Jordan Blum. "I think it's more of a trial and error, and the positive results help with how you attack the problem next time. I don't think it's confidence as much as learning how to move on productively, how to keep the plates spinning or be proactive instead of lingering in the failure or dwelling too long on the problem."

Berry, in fact, says he practices "lead with questions on a daily basis."

"Think of this. You are in a label meeting and the owner says, 'we have an artist that we really want to get famous.' You say, 'I think TikTok is huge, you gotta get her on TikTok.' The label owner shows you the door.

"Here is how that should have gone. The owner says, 'we have an artist that we really want to get famous.' You ask, 'Gotcha. Who is the artist, how old, what do you hope achieve with her fame?' Label owner says, 'She is 63, sings spiritual hymns and hosts a ministry in Africa.'

"If you had asked the right questions, you would have a much greater chance of giving valuable advice."

You can't do everything needed in the content process, and you can't do everything well. But you should over time develop confidence that you're asking the right questions, continually improving, learning from your mistakes, connecting with the right people, and surrounding yourself with people who fill your "gaps" while you perhaps fill some of theirs.

How about you? In what areas of your life's or career's activities do you feel more or less confident? During the YOU attribute, we briefly addressed your "knack"—those things that you naturally seem good at. Where does your knack(s) come from? How did it develop? Why do you feel a natural inclination to be "good" at that ability? Have you practiced it over time? Did/does someone help encourage you to believe in your knack? Is your knack more specific to a task (e.g., learning/applying a new software) or more general (e.g., ability to engage well with people)? You may come to realize that your knack is more applicable to the things you'll "need" in order to succeed in media-related professions than may appear on the surface.

This is why *knowing yourself* is so critical in life and in career in the collaborative media professions. When you have an accurate self-assessment of your relative strengths and weaknesses, you're in a better position to move forward in concert with your interests and talents. You gain clarity about not only what matters to you but also what you need to work on connected to your interests, and also *who* you need to connect with to help you be more effective. You'll gain confidence over time in your abilities to achieve almost anything because you'll actively absorb new skills and connect with the right people. You'll undoubtedly make some mistakes along the way, but you'll learn from them and keep moving forward.

Think about a "team" you've worked with that functioned particularly well together. This could be a production, an organization, a sport, etc. Did you all have the same strengths? Did you all perform the same roles, or did you "fill gaps" in key ways? In my experience, the best "teams" often have players with a variety of skills and attributes, serving complementary roles to create a whole greater than the sum of the individual parts.

FOUR WAYS TO BOOST YOUR CONFIDENCE[1]

Albert Bandura believed that self-efficacy is developed through four domains: Mastery, Vicarious Experience, Verbal Persuasion, and Emotional Self-Regulation. Below are four ways to boost your confidence:

1. *Celebrate Your Success* (Mastery). Work on setting goals that are achievable, but not necessarily easy. When you succeed at something, you are able to build a powerful belief in your ability.
2. *Observe and Emulate Others* (Vicarious Experience). Seeing others of perceived related ability put in effort and succeeding can increase your belief in your own ability to succeed.
3. *Seek Positive Affirmations* (Verbal Persuasion). Positive feedback from friends, peers, mentors, and people you respect can help you feel greater confidence in your own abilities.
4. *Encourage Yourself* (Emotional Self-Regulation). Replace negativity with positive self-talk that promotes self-belief.

The important thing here is that you don't need to have high confidence in every single function related to your work and career goals, but you need to develop confidence that you're surrounding yourself (as much as you can at any point in time) with people you can confidently rely on, while developing the specific skills most relevant to what you want to do.

"I have learned to master the art of providing more value to those I work with than they provide me in early relationship building and with less ask of their time," says Berry. "I know people that lead every convo with 'what ya gonna pay me.' Those people are still broke. I know people that said, 'sure, don't worry about the pay, let's get this right first.' Those people run the biggest companies in entertainment."

What Successful Media Professionals "Master" to Become Confident

Albert Bandura believed that "mastery" of skills and goals is the single most powerful way to gain self-belief in one's abilities.[2] I asked several successful media and entertainment professionals in a range of areas and experience levels what they "needed to master" in order to become confident in their work. The answers might surprise you.

Production Coordinator. A huge part of my job now is handling "deliverables." This is something that absolutely terrified me because I am not what they call "tech-savvy." As a Production Coordinator, it is my job to ensure that the production company is delivering the right materials (text and textless master cuts, snap ins, sneak peeks, promos—the list gets scarier and scarier) on the correct deadline and ensuring it fits with network's guidelines. I abused my boss's statement, "You can ask me anything!" and was in his office over and over again until I felt confident enough to handle on my own. It didn't happen overnight and I made some mistakes, but I finally got there. Now, I feel so confident that I can practically do it with my eyes closed!

ATTRIBUTE TIP FOR CAREER SUCCESS

Fake It 'Til You Make It

"I swear, employers can smell insecurities from a mile away," says Marissa Donovan, a young entertainment professional in New York. "Now, everyone has them, but you mask it as much as you can because you want your team to believe that no matter what they throw at you, what the deadline is, or what it will take to complete, you'll get it done and you'll get it done right. It all starts with how you present yourself right out of the gate. First days are absolutely nerve racking and causes sensory overload, trust me, I know!"

Faking it 'til you make it does *not* imply that you should fabricate your abilities and you should *never* promise a skill that you literally cannot deliver. However, while you should not expect to know or understand every intricacy of a new job, you *should have confidence that you can figure out how to do almost anything* and will devote the time and energy needed to do it well (including asking good questions to make sure you do things correctly). It's important to remember that you received your job or internship because someone believes you have the skills to accomplish the tasks required of the position.

And that part *is* real.

Marissa further explains how this approach can be transformative. "The miraculous part is, as I continue with a project and realize it's not as hard as I thought it was going to be or that I've found the right tools to help, my confidence actually does go up," she says. "So, in the end, I no longer have to fake it. My employers and coworkers see that enough times and they want me to be on their project because the proof is in the pudding. Confidence has helped me develop and has given me opportunities I did not think I would have."

Hip-Hop Artist/Producer. For me, the most important thing was just figuring out my roles as a producer/writer/artist; what I'm good at, what I'm not the best at, and so on, and building relationships with the right people to fill in those blanks. I realized that I started connecting with more musicians who are amazing at the things I lacked confidence in, started inviting them to the sessions and I found myself completely confident in the job at hand. This continues to lead to more opportunities and work.

Producer. Two skills I had to master that go hand in hand are speaking out and pitching ideas. In creative meetings, I did have the tendency to let the "adults" speak because I thought I was too green and that my ideas probably weren't very good anyway. This, of course, is a lack of self-confidence! Without fail, someone would speak out during a meeting and share the same thought I had. Instead of getting booed out of the meeting, it was well received! Afterward, I would feel regret for not speaking up sooner. I had to remind myself that I was hired for a reason—my bosses saw potential in me and knew what I was capable of. I no longer shut myself down before I even give my ideas a chance, and it feels great!

TV Reporter. I had to master focusing on what I can offer rather than what I was lacking in order to feel confident. Every day I choose to focus on my strengths, while identifying and working to improve my weaknesses.

Post-Production Supervisor. Earlier in my career, technical skills were more important as the technology was so young, but as a producer, the soft/people skills became very important, very quickly. In a high-stress production situation, where everything is going wrong, the producer needs to be the calm in the middle of the storm. Projecting confidence and having the skills to solve the problem and enlist the team to pull it off is the job and exuding that confidence is the key to success.

Non-Scripted Producer. Communication is the biggest soft skill I had to master to feel more confident in my work. And under the big umbrella of communication, I feel interpersonal communication and listening are the more specific skills that have helped. . . . And writing is probably the most important hard skill to have. I write interview questions, bites, hot sheets, papercuts, voiceover and narration, and take field notes. Honing these hard skills has definitely helped build my confidence.

Post-Production Coordinator. Communication. It's understanding when to communicate, what to communicate about, the most precise and politically appropriate way to communicate, and whom to communicate to. That may sound overwhelming, but those things start to become clearer as you learn the structure and intricacies of your particular position.

As you can see through these examples, being good and reliable with the "hard skills" are important in specific situations (and you're more than smart enough to learn them), but the softer skills of communication and relationship maintenance are perhaps even more critical to gain confidence in a collaborative world.

The Pathway to Gaining Confidence: Enjoy the Process

Have you ever been around with someone who works really hard and also exhibits a certain joy about their work? These individuals are actually putting on display for you a key element of acquiring confidence and the successes that often ensue: they *enjoy the process*!

Our culture is one that focuses on outcomes and results. They *are* important in the day-to-day activities found in your profession. However, strict focus on outcomes in your development often shortcuts the many benefits found within the process.

Look at the following definitions connected to "enjoying a process":

Enjoy: (1) To take pleasure or satisfaction, and (2) to have for one's use, benefit, or lot, and (3) to experience with joy (and some synonyms: adore, delight in, dig, rejoice, relish, revel, savor).

Process: natural phenomenon marked by gradual changes that lead toward a particular result.

Experience: knowledge or practical wisdom gained from what one has observed, encountered, or undergone.

ATTRIBUTE TIP FOR CAREER SUCCESS

Give Good Physiology

Actress Blake Lively says, "The most beautiful thing you can wear is confidence." There's a lot of truth to that!

Body language communicates so much about your confidence (or lack thereof). So be aware of your physiology and the impact it can have on how confident people perceive you to be—and how confident *you* feel.

Smile, stand up straight, square your shoulders, open up your chest, carry yourself with good posture, breathe deeply, walk with a purposeful stride, look people in the eye. (And don't forget to smile.) Make these actions a habit. You'll feel better and you'll look better to others.

The positive effect of your positive physiology is threefold: (1) you will naturally feel more confident with good body language, and (2) people will tend to respond to you more favorably, which in turn (3) will increase your own feelings of self-confidence.

If this is something you don't do particularly well or haven't consciously applied, *practice it*! This might feel a little awkward at first, but it's a habit worth developing to enhance your ongoing confidence and self-efficacy.

If you engage with your career (and life) experiences with joy, do you think people will be drawn to you? Will they more likely seek you out when opportunities present themselves? Free yourself from doubt by enjoying the process of your development, and trust that positive things will happen, even if the exact outcomes can't be fully predicted and the road is bumpy at times. Confidence is not a switch that's flipped, although it may feel like that when you've developed it and are applying to specific situations. When your aims are directed toward something meaningful to you, you will be more open, even excited, to develop new skills and engage receptively with an open spirit. You'll be excited to share what you know and also seek to learn more from people connected to your interests.

When have you been more inclined to "enjoy a process"? What does this tell you about you and what's truly meaningful to you? When we enjoy the process, our general orientation is to be happy/joyful *in the middle of it*, working hard to get things done, but less focused on strict outcomes than what you're learning and developing in the process. The resulting confidence you gain in this process can be powerful. "When you have confidence, you can have a lot of fun. And when you have fun, you can do amazing things," says football legend Joe Namath.

Will you enjoy the process of every career-related pursuit? No. Will you enjoy every aspect of your daily work? Of course not. But if your general orientation leans toward enjoying the process, especially for the things that matter to you, you will be in better position to see more of the forest and not just the trees, and this will become very beneficial to your confidence and to *you* in The Big Picture.

I *wish* I could state that I enjoyed the entire process of writing this book. But that's simply not true. Although I strongly believe in the book's concept,

I did not always believe in my ability to execute it. I had never written a book before and wondered if I could actually follow all the way through. I struggled at times with how to approach certain parts. I procrastinated. I made excuses, real and made up. That's not easy for me to admit, but it's the truth.

How did it change? When I realized it was *meaningful to me* and that by putting myself through the process I would gain skills, learn about myself, and hopefully help others *in the process*. I stopped worrying about making every page perfect and allowed myself to rely on the expertise of others and not feel like I have to know everything. (The reason I like being a teacher is because I love to learn!) So I came to believe I would figure it out, and I became more confident in the process.

I also remembered that when things have worked out best for me are times when I've enjoyed the process, did things because I was drawn to them, challenged by them, and willing to work harder because I enjoyed engaging with them. I could even find humor in the most humorless topics. I found ways to keep going because they were meaningful to me. Employing the Multiple Benefits Paradigm (from the Persistent attribute) helped me focus on "why."

Enjoying the process doesn't make things "easy," but it does make things *better*. When you enjoy the process of your own development, you will offer to yourself and others more positive energy, you'll connect better with people, and your efforts will more often move forward in concert with what matters to you. People with confidence are willing to weather the bumps in the road and relish the potentials for growth and development they offer. Otherwise you'll reduce the joy in the result, because you're working strictly toward an outcome rather than toward your own personal growth. A "growth mindset" helps you gain confidence over time.

You have everything it takes to be successful. Your belief in your abilities is a strong determinant of the efforts you will exert to become extraordinary. So remember to . . .

—challenge yourself to master tasks relevant to your interests and aspirations;
—closely observe those who are succeeding in the ways you want to succeed;
—surround yourself with people who believe in you and affirm your abilities to succeed; and
—be encouraging to yourself.

CONFIDENCE Exercises

1. Find and make a study of (e.g., via observation and/or interview) a role model whose success and example will aid your own development and confidence. Ideally, this person has a few more years of experience working in an area connected to your interests. How does the role model approach their work? What are *specific* things you observe or learn that you can apply now and going forward?

2. What do you believe you are "naturally" good at (or your "knack(s)")? What do they tell you about your core abilities—and beliefs about your abilities?

3. Set an achievable (though not necessarily easy) goal to "master" a hard skill relevant to your interests and aspirations. How will attainment of this goal help boost your confidence?

4. Describe a situation where you *enjoyed the process* of reaching a goal or aim. How did you approach the obstacles/challenges in ways that were different from other situations when you perhaps did not enjoy the process? How could your understanding of your approach be of benefit to you in your professional pursuits?

5. Identify people in your relationship network that serve to increase your self-efficacy—who have encouraged you and communicated a belief in you. Send each a thank you note, expressing gratitude for how they are making a difference in your life.

Resilience

A positive, adaptive response in the face of significant adversity

<u>Synonyms</u>: Buoyant, Tough, Thick Skin, Irrepressible

<u>Antonyms</u>: Delicate, Weak, Rigid, Helpless

All the adversity I've had in my life, all my troubles and obstacles, have strengthened me. . . . You may not realize it when it happens, but a kick in the teeth may be the best thing in the world for you.

—Walt Disney

I was fired from my first job after college. I worked as a reporter and camera person at a TV station in Springfield, Missouri. The work conditions were terrible, as was our product (in the newsroom we derisively called it "I Missed It News," instead of our branded "Eyewitness News"). In particular, the station's owner and GM was perhaps the most uncaring human being I have met—to this day. He only cared about money and paid very low (minimum) wages. The work environment was toxic, morale was beyond low, and he treated people poorly and unfairly.

About five months into the job, the GM mandated that each of his reporters produce *FIVE* news stories *per day*. You don't need to know a lot about news production or journalism to understand that this is laughably impossible—not to mention completely unnecessary. We aired only two thirty-minute newscasts per day, which, taking out commercials, weather, and sports, amounted to about thirty minutes *total* of actual news content. With five reporters required to produce five news packages per day (most roughly two minutes in length), you also don't have to be a math genius to calculate that a lot of stories would never make it to the air—and those that did were of poor quality because we had to spit out (an appropriate phrase) so many stories to meet the quota.

At a certain point amid this insanity, I decided that I would produce two "quality" news packages per day, do the best I could on those and let the cards fall where they may. Well, they fell all right! After a few days undetected, the GM realized that I was not meeting the daily quota. He called me in, berated me for being insubordinate (which I guess I was), told me my father must not have shown me a good work ethic (definitely *not* true), and then fired me on the spot.

At the moment, this was very painful. *Very*. Even though I was making minimum wage and in a bad situation, this was my first job out of college and I had never been fired from anything. *Painful*.

But just one day later I had a sudden revelation that's had a major impact on my life: I realized that if I become the exact *opposite* of the person who fired me—I treat people fairly and with kindness; I don't exploit others for personal gain—my life will turn out okay. I didn't have a clue where life was going to lead me and I didn't even have a job (and needed every dollar to make ends meet), but I gained a measure of genuine comfort and empowerment with this choice.

Very painful then. Wouldn't trade the experience for anything now.

The fact of the matter is that being fired—especially in this manner and by *this person*—was one of the best things that ever happened to me. I'm actually *thankful and grateful* that this happened the way that it did, when it did. It helped form who I am to this day and, though I'm far from perfect, I gained a compelling notion of what I wanted to be through what I didn't want to be. When I've faced challenges or disappointments since then, I'm comforted in the belief that there's something important to learn, even when I might not know what that is at the moment.

ATTRIBUTE TIP FOR CAREER SUCCESS

Embrace Anti-Models (You'll Learn What *Not* to Do)

Some of the most powerful lessons you will learn come from realizing what not to do. If, that is, you're paying attention. One of my very favorite episodes of *Seinfeld* is called "The Opposite." George concludes that things "just aren't working" for him and decides to do the opposite of his "every instinct toward judgment and common sense that I've ever had." So, he does the opposite. He gets a date with a beautiful woman after telling her, "I'm unemployed and live with my parents," and gets a dream job with the New York Yankees after angrily telling bombastic owner George Steinbrenner that he has "ruined this glorious franchise all to the service of your massive ego" (upon which Steinbrenner says, "Hire this man!").

I think the reason this episode is particularly noteworthy for me is the idea that you *will* interact with some people who don't have your best interests at heart, don't treat you and others with respect or kindness, perform in some way ineffectively and inefficiently. You'll have bosses or a "superior" who is clearly not *superior*. They may treat you unfairly, even harshly. Allow yourself to feel the frustration, even anger, of this but also learn what not to do and how *not* to be.

Be the Opposite.

Many of the best, most impactful, learning experiences come from the pain of what not to do. You can actually gain a lot from these people, so learn what you can (i.e., *not* to do) from these situations as a way to make distinctions to better yourself. The anti-models, just like the positive role models and mentors, can teach you a lot. Find ways to learn from the experience rather than dismiss them. They will serve to reinforce your own integrity and core values.

By the way, I was fired from my second job, too. This one was far less acrimonious—I was "let go" by really good people—and the firing was more like a mercy killing. I worked as a radio station salesperson and made *zero* sales in two months. A terrible fit for my interests and personality, it was nonetheless "in the industry" and I needed a job. Being "let go" a second time was also painful and even more disillusioning, but I hung in there. After a few months of unemployment—a couple of temp jobs here and there—I landed a position at an advertising agency, and my career began to take shape.

Two firings within the first year of a marriage can put strain on any relationship. But, fortunately and significantly, my young wife was a rock of support and continued to believe in me even as we struggled for months, living paycheck to paycheck on her first-year teacher's salary.

Embrace the Struggle, Don't Run from It

Resilience is such an important attribute for your career in the media professions, not to mention a critical life skill. Being resilient is much more than "hanging in there" during difficult times or developing "thick skin." Just as weights provide resistance to build muscle in your body, resilience does the same to your mind and spirit, empowering you to do and be more than you thought possible. Resilience helps you grow, *seasons* you, and helps *reinforce* who you really are as you continue to move forward.

We all face personal and professional setbacks, and no one *wants* to struggle (you're a masochist if you do). But struggle offers an opportunity to reveal our true aspirations and character. Successful media professionals are often "grateful" in retrospect that certain challenges, disappointments, and "failures" happened in the ways they did. Those who avoid struggle altogether rarely make these important distinctions. Even things that we never, *ever* "wish" to happen—for example, severe illness, tragedy—can nevertheless provide opportunities for learning and personal growth.

"Failing hurts. It's truly painful," says Herb Trawick, cohost of *Pensado's Place*. "When you're failing, that is your time of most acute learning. But failure teaches you something you'll never repeat, because you learn it wasn't good for you. So, the only context you can take from that is that you've learned something that will probably amplify you."

You've probably heard the phrase "Those who succeed the most have failed the most." There is a lot truth in this statement. "Failure" to the resourceful, passionate, ambitious, persistent media professional is *fuel* to try again—to figure out a new, better way. Failure is never failure if viewed as an opportunity to learn or grow in some way. As J. K. Rowling once wrote, "It is impossible to live without failing at something, unless you live so cautiously that you might as well not have lived at all—in which case, you fail by default."

Young media professionals who lack the ability to handle disappointment and adversity are less likely to bounce back and move forward. That's why Resilience is a reinforcing attribute. You don't have to "like" being in the middle of the struggle or adversity, but your broader Big Picture viewpoint should be to embrace the struggle because in the fight to get where you are going (wherever that is), you'll become stronger, smarter, tougher. You'll be more resourceful, better able to adapt, and more able to persist. This important component of self-efficacy will lead you to be an even better *you*.

Think about it. Do you *really* want to skate through life with no challenges or obstacles? Is that really the "best" thing for you? How many successful media professionals do you know who didn't encounter struggle or obstacles? Don't be fooled. (As mentioned earlier, the popular press often makes the process seem far too easy.) Virtually every extraordinary media professional has struggled at times, faced setback, been told no, been treated unfairly, got passed over, and/or had a "sure thing" fall through.

Those who are successful and seem happy are *not* that because everything came easily. They are happy because they're doing things that they are passionate about and are excited to engage with on a daily basis. They're also happy *because* of the struggle and not for not having to struggle. They knew they grew from the struggle and wouldn't be the same person today had those struggles not occurred.

Resilience and Your Response-ability

COVID-19 offered all of us an extreme and unwanted challenge. Media and entertainment professionals are normally somewhat immune to severe economic times (people seek entertainment more when times are tough). However, with the possible exception of the news industry, even entertainment professionals suffered greatly because many people literally could not work together (in a physical sense). The resilient ones will be okay in the aftermath, and some might seize opportunities within the challenges presented. Others won't be so fortunate.

As resilience is cited by the workforce as an "essential top factor" for career success, the question becomes "how?" and "why?" The military often refers to resilience as "intestinal fortitude" (i.e., gutting it out). But for most of us, developing resilience involves multiple genetic and, especially, environmental factors. "[Resilience] emerges at the intersection of a range of skills and attitudes," says Professor Marcus O'Donnell. "We tend to think of resilience as some kind of private, secret power but actually resilience is something we learn by carefully analyzing what's happening to us and actively crafting a response."[1]

Three key factors promote psychological resilience:[2]

1. *Internal support*: Abilities and skills such as communication, problem-solving, behavioral and emotional regulation, hope, and a positive view of oneself.
2. *External support*: Caring, supportive relationships with friends, family, colleagues, peers, and the like.
3. *Existential support*: Cultural values and faith/belief systems.

All three are important, but I direct your attention to the second factor. *We need people in our lives!* Your relationship network (see Connective) is particularly important for media professionals, especially when times get tough. These "tight" connections can offer new opportunities to help you get back on your feet. If you have others who believe in you and want to work with you, you will be in much better position to bounce back. Your demonstrated ability to persist and your personal integrity will allow—even encourage—you to recover from adversity more quickly and effectively. Your relationship network—both in and out of the industry—becomes all the more important.

TOP TEN CHARACTERISTICS OF RESILIENT PROFESSIONALS[3]

1. *Confident*: feel confident in their own skins and give themselves permission to take appropriate risks.
2. *Adaptable*: mentally and emotionally flexible, which helps them deal with the relentless onslaught of tasks, interactions, and information.
3. *Emotionally intelligent*: manage emotions with skill such that they are responsive not reactive when relating to others.
4. *Social*: loving family and good friendships make people more stress-resistant and less likely to get sick. It diminishes the impact of difficulties and increase the feelings of self-worth and self-confidence.
5. *Optimistic*: see glass is half full and believe that biggest setbacks often bring the greatest breakthroughs. They don't enjoy hardship but find wisdom in the experience.
6. *Playful*: seek fun in all tasks, not afraid of making mistakes, can laugh at themselves.
7. *Intuitive*: trust their gut feeling and go with what feels most true and authentic in each situation.
8. *Compassionate*: empathetic listeners and compassionate responders.
9. *Mindful*: have strong sense of self, nurtured through finding time to engage in contemplation exercises.
10. *Kaizen*: daily commitment to continuous improvement so they look for ways to increase their well-being, happiness, productivity, efficiency, and a capacity for excellence. They rapidly assimilate new and unexpected experiences.

The key is how you *respond* to the struggles and difficulties. Do you wallow in self-pity, perhaps conditioned by "learned helplessness," or do you become more determined to prove people wrong? Do you at least learn what *not* to do?

Resilience leads to a greater desire to persist toward any goal because your response will not "keep you down." These are all choices we make, even if we sometimes don't consciously realize it. We all know people who *don't* respond productively to struggles and unfairness. And we know a few who do.

Viktor Frankl has been an obvious inspiration for this book, as he has for countless books and millions of people. Frankl, who suffered almost unimaginable indignities and hardship in Nazi concentration camps, states that you can have everything taken away except one thing: your freedom to choose your response and your attitude. It's the last of the human freedoms. The classic *7 Habits of Highly Effective People*, drawing from Dr. Frankl, states that your *response* to what happens to you is more important than what happens to you.[4] As self-aware humans, we have the *ability* to choose our response. Is it a productive choice that allows you to move on and forward, or does it continue to limit you and your choices/opportunities? These are important questions to answer when you face personal and professional disappointment.

So how do we *condition ourselves* for a productive response when we face struggle and adversity?

An expectation for positive outcomes, even in the middle of adversity, is at the top of the list for many who study and observe resilience. For example, Wu et al. lists "realistic optimism" as a top factor and also includes high-coping self-efficacy (confidence and adaptability), high cognitive functioning (changing one's views to find meaning), emotional regulation, strong social skills and social network, positive identity, humor and positive thinking, and a sense of altruism (generosity).[5] Notice how many of the attributes you're developing are needed to enact your resilience.

Resilient people face difficult situations realistically, yet find ways to be optimistic. "I think so many experiences and jobs have showed me what I'm good at (and not so good at), and where I have a passion that allows me to stretch and try new things," says Sarah Herbert, a former student and shining example of realistic optimism. "There is always something to learn from what we lose out on. It can make us stronger and more focused if we are open to new directions and different opportunities."

The extraordinary media professional, who faces these types of challenges more than most, *grows* from the disappointment and challenges. Therein is the locus for critical distinctions that helps fuel the attainment of your aspirations. And the things you don't "get" may even lead to unexpected, exciting directions and outcomes that you can't yet visualize. Embrace the adventure your resilience can bring.

Life is a marathon, not a sprint. You'll travel down many roads. There will be some peaks and valleys along the way. Extraordinary media professionals thrive over the long haul. Their suitcases are packed with key attributes to help them navigate the paths ahead. They, in the words of Harvey Mackay, "understand that life can be a bumpy road, but at least it is leading somewhere."

In 2019, my wife, Pat, died of cancer. This was easily the saddest, most traumatic experience of my life as I watched my partner of thirty-six years suffer through months of illness and unsuccessful treatments. The mother of our two children, who stood by me when I was fired (twice), Pat was always a vital source of support as I tried to figure out my life. She sacrificed far more than me through our constant moves for my career, including for a program in LA while she held down the fort in Ohio six months of the year. I miss her terribly.

And yet I've found paths to purpose and meaning. All I needed to do was look for them.

My mother and I endowed a scholarship in Pat's name to help future Ohio University students. I'm so grateful that I had the opportunity to give this gift to Pat on her birthday, in a Columbus hospital, two months before her passing. I will always cherish the look of surprise, happiness, and characteristic humility on Pat's face as she opened a card revealing the scholarship.

Pat had struggled to pay for college, so knowing she would have an enduring role in helping others pay for their education meant the world to her.
And that meant the world to me.

Family, friends, and students helped me in ways big and small. All were
consequential. I think of my media students in LA as I made constant trips
back and forth to Ohio during the summer of 2019 as my daughter Kaatie,
sister-in-law Lynn Wilson, and father-in-law Tom Butcher made sure that Pat
was taken care of while I attended to my job. These amazing, life-affirming
students were so kind, adaptable, and empathetic throughout this difficult
period, while continuing to pursue their own dreams.

On July 24, through tears I couldn't hold back, I told my class that the
decision had been unexpectedly made to place my wife in hospice care,
necessitating an overnight flight back to Ohio to oversee her transport from
the Cleveland Clinic to Athens. All twenty-eight students came up to me
after class and hugged me. Many told me that they loved me. At the end
of the program, they presented me a "scrapbook" of photos and memories
from our experience in LA with personalized thank you notes. Few posses-
sions mean more to me.

On August 24, one day before the fall LA program was to start, my wife
passed away peacefully in our home. My great friend Jen Jones Donatelli
flew to LA to help make sure our new students got off to a positive start.
At dinner with my new students upon arrival in LA, Sami Scholl announced
that the group had all chipped in to make a donation to Pat's scholarship.
This inspired me even more to focus my energies toward making this a
highly beneficial personal and professional experience for my students.

And this is how I will continue to honor my wife.

Yes, I had learned in the most personal way that even the most difficult,
stressful situations can offer opportunities for growth, clarity, and meaning-
fulness . . .

Our connections and connected-ness;
Our passions;
Our capacities to persist and adapt;
Our values and aspirations;
Our response-ability;
Our understanding of who we really are moving forward.

> *Indeed, this life is a test. It is a test of many things—of our convictions and*
> *priorities, our faith and our faithfulness, our patience and our resilience,*
> *and in the end, our ultimate desires.*
>
> —Sheri L. Dew

RESILIENCE Exercises

1. List *three* people (e.g., family, friend, and peer) you know who will "have
   your back" when/if you face significant adversity. Then describe (1) *why*
   each person is meaningful to you and (2) *how*, specifically, you know
   you'll have this important support. (And will you reciprocate if/when
   those key supporters face adversity?)

2. Describe a person you know who embodies resilience. What is his or her story? What characteristics does the person demonstrate in the face of significant adversity? How might your observations aid your own resilience or ability to bounce back from difficulties?

3. Describe a difficult, challenging, and/or awkward situation you've encountered at your job/internship. How did you handle the situation? What did you learn from your experience that will benefit you going forward?

4. Describe the *worst* job/work-related experience you ever had. What made this job "bad"? What did you learn about yourself and what you do (and *don't*) want to do *or be* as a result of this experience?

5. Describe the biggest challenge or setback you've overcome. What did you learn about yourself, your values, and your capabilities by overcoming this challenge? (Use the "Defining Moments" exercise from the YOU attribute to help develop your answer.) In what ways did you employ "realistic optimism" to help you overcome this challenge?

The 13th Attribute

Luck

The force that seems to operate for good or ill in a person's life, as in shaping circumstances, events, opportunities

Over the years, hundreds of successful media professionals have expressed to me how "luck" played a key part in their career success and how "lucky" they feel to be doing what they're doing. This is never stated with false modesty. It's real and genuine.

And I know each has worked really hard to get where they are.

So what's really going on?

Although some degree of serendipity occurs for many who experience good fortunate or get a "break" in the media professions, I find that luck is rarely of the "tap-on-the-shoulder, out-of-left-field" variety, but rather the internalization of many, if not all, of the 12 Attributes found in this book converted to action in the service of their ambitions and passions.

"Lucky" media professionals don't feel this way because they've had it easy or never faced challenges. To the contrary, they've worked hard and smart with amazing focus, made their share of mistakes (even "failed"—sometimes a *lot*), and yet are able and willing—even driven—to keep moving forward. They remain open to new opportunities and see challenges as opportunities. They proactively enact upon their immediate environments, connecting with key people who see a consistency in approach and yet have the ability to "roll with" changes. Individuals in their relationship network appear almost to be at work for them in ways they don't realize, which lead to unanticipated opportunities. These "lucky" people have reputations as solutions to problems rather than problems themselves and treat others with respect. They attract people through their passion and positive energy. They are interested and interest*ing*.

ATTRIBUTE TIP FOR CAREER SUCCESS

When You Help Others, You're Helping Yourself

The aforementioned heading is something I tell my students at the end of each program in LA. If you're willing to share what you know, you're not only enhancing bonds in your relationship network but also displaying confidence in yourself, your abilities, and your relationships. You're less likely to look at people as "competition," but rather as colleagues, and any competition that might ensue only serves to elevate your own game.

Holding info or contacts "close to the vest" detracts rather than enhances your opportunities in The Big Picture. It's a show of insecurity rather than self-belief. (You're not a pushover either.) However, when you willingly, openly share what you know (and *who* you know) with others, you're actually reinforcing your own opportunities with your relationship network.

What are some key ways to do this?

(1)   Introduce people you meet to others in your relationship network.
(2)   Share information openly—an insight you gained from someone, or perhaps read.
(3)   Devote your time—your most precious commodity—for a project/task to help someone you know.
(4)   Listen genuinely with empathy.

You'll be amazed by the ways this helps you in The Big Picture.

Is it any wonder these people experience luck in their lives? *Feel* lucky?

Being in the right place at the right time (e.g., your availability to work or meeting the right person at an opportune moment) does come into play at times, but these occurrences of "good luck" are undoubtedly enhanced by a good reputation and *readiness* to take on more advanced opportunities (or the first one) to service ongoing development.

"We found lucky and unlucky people have no insight into why they're lucky or not. But the lucky ones would tell us, 'I went to this party and chatted up these people.' The fact that they went to the party and explored commonalities, people they both knew, created opportunities for luck," says Bill Marvel of Knight Ridder Tribune News Service.

Oprah Winfrey puts it more directly: "I don't believe in luck. I think luck is preparation meeting opportunity."

Another reason I believe some successful media professionals ascribe their success to "luck" and "good fortune" is they see other talented, intelligent, "good" people who have not experienced the same types of success in the profession or no longer work in the media/creative professions at all. The other person didn't get the "breaks" they received.

A third reason successful media professionals feel lucky is because they followed their bliss, less concerned with practicality than with trusting what they are genuinely drawn to. As some others in their orbit couldn't understand why someone would embark on a career so unpredictable, and perhaps even dissuaded them from doing so, they "hung in" by trusting their own value system. They saw others working at jobs inside and outside the media industry that they weren't passionate about. Even as some others made more money faster, they trusted that the money (whatever it is) would eventually follow and you earned it in the process of your development.

I believe careers in the media and creative professions—the *content* professions—offer unsurpassed opportunity for self-actualization. Extraordinary media professionals become who they truly are. Few people have the great fortune to experience that.

"Find work that doesn't feel like work to you," my dad repeatedly told me as a child.

This simple, magical piece of advice reveals a key secret to life and success in The Big Picture: when your time and efforts are directed toward pursuits that don't feel like work *to you*, you'll be more likely to commit yourself toward that work, as well as the skills you need to develop, and enjoy more of the journey. You'll be at peace with your decisions and directions, even if you stray off the path from time to time.

If you are in pursuit of what's meaningful to you, *you are lucky* because what ensues will be richer than the sum of the individual successes and failures.

If you're doing things centrally for reasons other than money or title, *you are lucky.*

If you are in pursuit of things that make you come alive (even if every day isn't perfect), *you are lucky.*

If you have built deep relationships with people in and out of the industry, *you are lucky.*

If you seek to pay it forward (at least eventually) by helping others to develop their skills and attributes to successfully navigate these unpredictable industries, *you, too, will feel lucky.*

This book is an attempt to help us make more sense of these crazy, amazing professions and how your personal attributes can help be of service to you, your passions, and your ambitions. In the process, we also make more sense of life itself, and the successes that will ensue.

I hope you feel lucky, too.

LUCK Exercises

1. Describe a DM for you that came because of serendipity or being at the right place at the right time. What impact, if any, did you have to help make this a "lucky" occurrence?
2. What is a simple act you could do *today*—for example, devote your time, offer money, or share a contact—to make someone feel lucky? Commit to following through with this simple act of kindness.

Acknowledgments

And on the subject of being lucky . . .

I am so very fortunate for the support and expertise of my editor, Natalie Mandziuk. She was incredibly kind and patient with me as I worked through the loss of my wife. I appreciate your guidance for making *The 12 Attributes* a reality.

Thanks to Elizabeth Swayze for your belief in the book from its inception and for your confidence-building during the early chapters. My gratitude to Sylvia Landis, Patricia Stevenson, Jasti Bhavya, and Kim Lyons for all of your work during editorial, production, and marketing.

My fondest wish for anyone who reads this book is that you have a friend in your life as great as Tang Tang. A collaborator on early attributes research, Tang's belief in this book carried me through to the finish line. Her friendship means more than words can express.

My appreciation to colleagues in the School of Media Arts and Studies and the Scripps College of Communication at Ohio University. You've heard about this project for far too long. I'm happy it came to fruition.

Thanks to the thousands of students I've been blessed to work with during the past three decades. I've learned more from you than you've learned from me. Special thanks to the hundreds of students I've worked with in LA. The opportunity to observe your development on a daily basis accelerated my understanding and articulation of the 12 Attributes. It's my great joy to watch your successes now and in the future. I'm privileged to be a part of your life.

Thanks to hundreds of media and creative professionals that I have been able to learn from since I asked my simple question. Your passion and integrity inspire me. I am especially grateful to Terrell Boaz, Jen Jones Donatelli, Marissa Donovan, Hope Groves, Kevin Hamburger, Daniel Mondschain, and Paul Schneider for your time, feedback, and encouragement during various phases of this project.

If you've read this book, you already know the influence of my dad, Grover Cooper, who passed away in 2016. Of equal importance is my mom, Euva Cooper. It's an amazing thing to have someone in your life who believes in you so fiercely. Thank you for always supporting me and for encouraging me to be who I am.

Kaatie and Jac are most big-hearted individuals a parent could ever hope to raise. Your resilience and openness to people of all backgrounds make me very, very proud.

And Pat. I'll always look up to you in The Big Picture.

Notes

Introduction

1 "8 College Degrees with the Worst Return on Investment," accessed December 15, 2020, https://www.salary.com/articles/8-college-degrees-with-the-worst-return-on-investment/.

2 See Lee B. Becker, Tudor Vlad, Heidi Hennink-Kaminski, and Amy Jo Coffey, "2003–2004 Enrollment Report: Growth in Field Keeps Up with Trend," *Journalism & Mass Communication Educator* 59 (autumn 2004): 278–308; Roger Cooper and Tang Tang, "Gender and the Perceived Attributes for Career Success in the Media Industries," *Journal of Media Education* 3 (January 2012): 5–22.

The 12 Attributes

1 Definitions, synonyms, and antonyms were selected by referencing to dictionary.com, merriam-webster.com, and thesaurus.com.

2 Roger Cooper and Tang Tang, "The Attributes for Career Success in the Mass Communication Industries: A Comparison of Current and Aspiring Professionals," *Journalism and Mass Communication Educator* 65 (spring 2010): 40–55.

3 Quotes were from various searches connected to the attributes, including Google and brainyquotes.com, and the author's formal interviews and informal conversations with media professionals.

Part I

1 Viktor E. Frankl, *Man's Search for Meaning* (Boston, MA: Beacon Press, 1992), XIV–XV.

2 Alexandra Sifferlin. "Here's How Happy Americans Are Right Now," *Times*, last modified July 26, 2017, https://time.com/4871720/how-happy-are-americans/.

Attribute #1

1 Rachel Stowe Master. "David Alan Hall: A Name behind Hollywood Favorites," *TCU Magazine*, last modified winter 2019, https://magazine.tcu.edu/winter-2019/david-alan-hall-hollywood-ghostwriter/.

2 Malcolm Gladwell, "The 10,000-Hour Rule" in *Outliers: The Story of Success* (New York: Back Bay Books, 2011), 35–69.

Attribute #2

1 See Jeff Slayton, "Too Many Bodies: A Powerful Music Video That Fosters Change," *LA Dance Chronicle*, last modified September 28, 2018, https://www.ladancechronicle.com/too-many-bodies-a-powerful-music-video-that-fosters-change/; "Director Biography—Reena Dutt (Too Many Bodies)," *Experimental Film & Music Video Festival*, last modified August 13, 2019, https://experimentalfilmfestival.com/2019/08/13/director-biography-reena-dutt-too-many-bodies/.

2 Dayton Moore and Matt Fulks, *More than a Season: Building a Championship Culture* (Chicago, IL: Triumph Books, 2016).

3 Dean Keith Simonton, *Great Psychologists and Their Times: Scientific Insights into Psychology's History* (Washington, DC: Amer Psychological Association, 2002).

4 John L. Holland, "A Theory of Vocational Choice," *Journal of Counseling Psychology* 6(1) (1959): 35–45.

5 See Cal Newport, "Beyond Passion: The Science of Loving What You Do," last modified January 23, 2010, https://www.calnewport.com/blog/2010/01/23/beyond-passion-the-science-of-loving-what-you-do/; Edward L. Deci and Richard M. Ryan, "Self-Determination Theory"

in *Handbook of Theories of Social Psychology*, eds. Paul A. M. Van Lange, Arie W. Kruglanski, and E. Tory Higgins (Thousand Oaks, CA: Sage Publications, 2012), 416–436.

6 See David Kadavy, "Science Confirms: Don't Find Your Passion. Grow It," last modified June 21, 2018, https://medium.com/the-mission/science-confirms-dont-find-your-passion-grow-it-c3b08e7e631b.

7 Paul A. O'Keefe, Carol S. Dweck, and Gregory M. Walton, "Implicit Theories of Interest: Finding Your Passion or Developing It," *Psychological Science* 29(10) (September 2018): 1653–1664.

8 Joshua Moore and Helen Glasgow, *The Growth Mindset: A Guide to Professional and Personal Growth* (Scotts Valley, CA: CreateSpace Independent Publishing, 2017).

Attribute #3

1 See "25 Benefits of Mentoring," accessed July 18, 2017, https://www.get.mentoringcomplete.com/blog/bid/82312/Management-Mentors-25-Benefits-of-Mentoring.

2 See "Success through Goal Setting," accessed April 20, 2018, https://www.briantracy.com/blog/personal-success/success-through-goal-setting-part-1-of-3/; John Kapeleris, "Only Three Percent of the Population Set Goals and Objectives," last modified January 18, 2016, https://www.linkedin.com/pulse/only-three-percent-population-set-goals-objectives-john-kapeleris.

3 Madhuleena Roy Chowdhury, "The Science & Psychology of Goal-Setting 101," last modified December 11, 2020, https://positivepsychology.com/goal-setting-psychology/; Marilyn Price-Mitchell, "Goal-Setting Is Linked to Higher Achievement," *Psychology Today*, last modified March 14, 2018, https://www.psychologytoday.com/us/blog/the-moment-youth/201803/goal-setting-is-linked-higher-achievement?fbclid=IwAR2f33MuVuaek d4UKLNlg6JO2qWED5160lc7dEuG8g3Gqby4017FhN8dSqc; John Traugott, "Achieving Your Goals: An Evidence-Based Approach," last modified August 26, 2014, https://www.canr.msu.edu/news/achieving_your_goals_an_evidence_based_approach?fbclid=IwAR3D axMgganLAo7WqY5xg5kBgWNJUD0NpCq-_pLOiPWbF6EDngPodU0cCfs.

4 Quincy Seale, "On the Importance of Goal Setting: 6 Reasons Why You Need to Set Goals," accessed March 7, 2019, https://www.keepinspiring.me/why-you-need-to-set-goals/.

Part II

1 Stephen R. Covey, *The 7 Habits of Highly Effective People: Powerful Lessons in Personal Change* (New York: Free Press, 2004).

2 Douglas J Brown, Richard T Cober, Kevin Kane, Paul E Levy, and Jarrett Shalhoop, "Proactive Personality and the Successful Job Search: A Field Investigation with College Graduates," *Journal of Applied Psychology* 91(3) (May 2006): 717–726; Scott E. Seibert, Maria L. Kraimer, and J. Michael Grant, "What Do Proactive People Do? A Longitudinal Model Linking Proactive Personality and Career Success," *Personal Psychology* 54(4) (December 2006): 845–874; Fu Yang Rebecca Chau, "Proactive Personality and Career Success," *Journal of Managerial Psychology* 31(2) (March 2016): 467–482.

Attribute #4

1 Eve Light Honthaner, *Hollywood Drive: What It Takes to Break in, Hang in & Make It in the Entertainment Industry* (New York: Routledge, 2018).

2 Master, "David Alan Hall."

Attribute #5

1 Covey, *The 7 Habits*.

2 See "The 80/20 Rule: Solving Board Problems with Pareto Analysis," accessed January 27, 2020, https://landing.directorpoint.com/blog/the-80-20-rule-solving-board-

problems-with-pareto-analysis/?fbclid=IwAR2jxBcS9YPtNTs7PR6Ov2-okkAp3M1xfX
Yo-AKShZKYk0vp7pDToBxVYJ8.
3 Sarah Richard, "7 Lessons about Creativity We Learned on Set with Robert Rodriguez,"
   last modified August 25, 2015, https://editorial.rottentomatoes.com/article/7-lessons-
   about-creativity-we-learned-on-set-with-robert-rodriguez/.
4 Richard, "7 Lessons."
5 Thomas Oppong, "For a More Creative Brain, Embrace Constraints," last modified
   November 30, 2017, https://www.inc.com/thomas-oppong/for-a-more-creative-brain-em
   brace-constraints.html.

Attribute #6

1 Katherine Greene and Richard Greene, *The Man behind the Magic: The Story of Walt
   Disney* (New York: Penguin Group, 1998).
2 "What Walt Disney Knew about Failure," last modified September 30, 2020, https://blogs.
   oracle.com/marketingcloud/what-walt-disney-knew-about-failure; Mactevirtute, "Persistence and Walt Disney," last modified February 10, 2013, https://mactevirtute.word
   press.com/2013/02/10/persistence-and-walt-disney/.
3 Tal Ben-Shahar, *Choose the Life You Want: The Mindful Way to Happiness* (New York:
   The Experiment, 2014).
4 See "7 Reasons Why Persistence Is the Key to Success," accessed June 4, 2020, http://www.
   magforliving.com/7-reasons-why-persistence-is-the-key-to-success/.
5 Carol S. Dweck, *Mindset: The New Psychology of Success* (New York: Ballantine Books,
   2007).
6 Thomas Oppong, "Persist. It Matters," last modified March 17, 2017, https://medium.
   com/personal-growth/persist-it-matters-7e4270f7c078.
7 Alyssa Maio, "What Is Persistence of Vision? Definition of an Optical Phenomenon,"
   last modified May 11, 2020, https://www.studiobinder.com/blog/what-is-persistence-
   of-vision-definition/.
8 Frankl, *Man's Search*.

Attribute #7

1 See Brian Grazer, "Curiosity Thrills This Cat," *AARP*, last modified September 2015,
   https://www.aarp.org/entertainment/television/info-2015/brian-grazer-celeb-news.html;
   Brian Grazer and Charles Fishman, *A Curious Mind: The Secret to a Bigger Life* (New
   York: Simon & Schuster, 2016).
2 See Grazer, "Curiosity Thrills This Cat."
3 Gary Wolf, "Steve Jobs: The Next Insanely Great Thing," *Wired*, last modified February 1,
   1996, https://www.wired.com/1996/02/jobs-2/.
4 *Walt: The Man behind the Myth*, directed by Jean-Pierre Isbouts (New York: Ballantine
   Books, 2007).
5 Celeste Kidd and Benjamin Hayden, "The Psychology and Neuroscience of Curiosity,"
   Neuron 88(3) (November 2015): 449–460.
6 Peter Skillen, "The Science of Passion Based Learning," last modified April 9, 2013,
   https://plpnetwork.com/2013/04/09/memorize-mesmerize/; Eleanor Duckworth, "Engaging Learners with Their Own Ideas: An Interview with Eleanor Duckworth," *A Foxfire
   journal for Teachers* 4(1) (Winter 1999): 28–30.
7 See Stephanie Vozza, "8 Habits of Curious People," last modified April 21, 2015, https://
   www.fastcompany.com/3045148/8-habits-of-curious-people?_ke=dHNvbWVydkBnbW
   FpbC5jb20%3D&utm_campaign=Taylor%20Somerville&utm_medium=email&utm_
   source=Revue%20newsletter; "Institute of Curiosity," accessed January 10, 2021, https://
   www.instituteofcuriosity.com.
8 Daniel H. Pink, *A Whole New Mind: Why Right-Brainers Will Rule the Future* (New York:
   The Penguin Group, 2006).
9 Vozza, "8 Habits."

10 Rebecca Muller, "How Improving Your 'Adaptability Quotient' Can Help You Succeed," last modified August 8, 2019, https://thriveglobal.com/stories/adaptability-quotient-cope-with-change-work-success/.

Attribute #8

1 Patrick Bateson, "Adaptability and Evolution," *Interface Focus* 7(5) (August 2017), https://doi.org/10.1098/rsfs.2016.0126.
2 Cooper and Tang, "The Attributes for Career Success," 47.
3 Jeff Boss, "14 Signs of an Adaptable Person," *Forbes*, last modified September 3, 2015, https://www.forbes.com/sites/jeffboss/2015/09/03/14-signs-of-an-adaptable-person/?sh=52815b1f16ea.
4 C. Rudolph, Kristi N. Lavigne, and H. Zacher, "Career Adaptability: A Meta-Analysis of Relationships with Measures of Adaptivity, Adapting Responses, and Adaptation Results," *Journal of Vocational Behavior* 98 (2017): 17–34.
5 Cooper and Tang, "The Attributes for Career Success," 46.
6 See Kara Cutruzzula, "These Days, Adaptability Is a Must-have Trait," last modified April 20, 2020, https://ideas.ted.com/these-days-adaptability-is-a-must-have-trait-heres-how-to-spot-it-and-increase-it/.
7 David Epstein, *Range: Why Generalists Triumph in a Specialized World* (New York: Riverhead Books, 2019).

Attribute #9

1 Cooper and Tang, "The Attributes for Career Success," 46.

Attribute #10

1 Charles H. Green, "Integrity: What's Up with That," last modified May 2, 2016, https://trustedadvisor.com/trustmatters/integrity-whats-up-with-that-2?fbclid=IwAR0baPmLs7A6Odrk9-DFqygDImq8eL98BTO2-bgm7vbjl_-RwgB0CU8tMK4#:~:text=The%20root%20of%20"integrity"%20is,whole%2C%20not%20fragmented%2C%20complete.
2 "Integrity: Definition and Examples," *Indeed*, last modified November 23, 2020, https://www.indeed.com/career-advice/career-development/integrity-at-work?fbclid=IwAR3Rq_oKF7CBJkaYeOYtt3YFvPq5zrHp2tlZLwQVZ6flI-e0dKG8GmmuMrI.

Part IV

1 Albert Bandura, *Self-Efficacy: The Exercise of Control* (New York: Worth Publishers, 1997).

Attribute #11

1 Kendra Cherry, "Self-Efficacy and Why Believing in Yourself Matters," last modified July 20, 2020, https://www.verywellmind.com/what-is-self-efficacy-2795954; Larry G. Maguire, "21 Ways to Boost Self-Efficacy and Achieve Your Goals," last modified October 11, 2019, https://medium.com/the-mission/21-ways-to-boost-self-efficacy-achieve-your-goals-9a1ba28dc0cc; Miriam Akhtar, "What Is Self-Efficacy? Bandura's 4 Sources of Efficacy Beliefs," *Positive Psychology,* last modified November 8, 2008 http://positivepsychology.org.uk/self-efficacy-definition-bandura-meaning/?fbclid=IwAR2mW2tRQtBKHNuqhckT7h9hVcEZtGQg5tgUelhaQkpUVJW5SjzOZ2Psj0c.
2 Bandura, *Self-Efficacy.*

Attribute #12

1 "How Resilience Can Lead to More Career Success," accessed December 8, 2020, https://this.deakin.edu.au/career/how-resilience-can-lead-to-more-career-success.

2   "Resilience: An Innate Human Capacity," accessed March 12, 2018, https://vawnet.org/sc/
resilience-innate-human-capacity?fbclid=IwAR1xlm57C7r1GxiBQy9acBH48S-L-IBub-
foIeRYeNw_uP1Htb8ZYFf_-5Kg#:~:text=But%20here%20is%20what%20we,on%20
the%20path%20to%20resilience.

3   Brad Waters, MSW, "10 Traits of Emotionally Resilient People," *Psychology Today*, last
modified May 21, 2013, https://www.psychologytoday.com/us/blog/design-your-path/20
1305/10-traits-emotionally-resilient-people.

4   Covey, *The 7 Habits*.

5   Jason H. Wu, Wayne K. Hoy, and C. John Tarter, "Enabling School Structure, Collective
Responsibility and a Culture of Academic Optimism: Toward a Robust Model of School
Performance in Taiwan," *Journal of Educational Administration* 51(2) (March 15, 2013):
176–193.

Index

Page references for figures are *italicized*.